Draught of His Majesty's Schooner
Sultana

Dimensions

| | |
|---|---|
| Length on the Range of Deck | 50'-6" |
| Keel for Tonnage | 38'-5⅝" |
| Breadth Moulded | 16'-0¾" |
| Depth in Hold | 8'-4" |
| Burthen in Tons | N° 52 $\frac{60}{94}$ |

The Sultana was purchased
for the British Navy in 1768.

Chapelle 1935

# Schooner *Sultana*

# Schooner *Sultana*

## Building a Chesapeake Legacy

Photographs by Lucian Niemeyer

Text by Drew McMullen

*With a foreword by John E. Swain*

Tidewater Publishers
Centreville, Maryland

Library of Congress Cataloging-in-Publication Data

Niemeyer, Lucian.
    Schooner Sultana : building a Chesapeake legacy / photographs by
Lucian Niemeyer ; text by Drew McMullen ; with a foreword by John E.
Swain.—1st ed.
        p. cm.
Includes bibliographical references and index.
    ISBN 0-87033-538-3 (hardcover)
    1. Sultana (Schooner)—Pictorial works. 2. Chestertown
(Md.)—History, Naval—20th century—Pictorial works. I. McMullen,
Drew, 1969- II. Title.
    VM311.F7 N54 2002
    623.8'2026—dc21
                                2002004193

The line drawing of *Sultana* that appears at the start of each chapter was drawn by John Poicus.

The drawings of *Sultana* shown on the inside front and back covers are by Howard I. Chapelle.
Courtesy of the Smithsonian Institution, NMAH/Transportation.

Printed in China
First edition

For Joyce Huber Smith, who gave and gave so that children might learn and the community would enjoy.

—L.N.

For Christian and Rosalind Havemeyer, for my entire *Sultana* family, and especially for my mother.

—D.M.

# Contents

*Schooner* **Sultana** *shipyard, May 2000*

# Foreword

As far back as I can remember I knew I wanted to build boats. The year 1966 found me in Oxford, Maryland, learning to build skipjack pleasure craft at Curtis Applegarth's yard. In 1968, I went to Dickerson Yachts in Trappe, Maryland, for two more years of learning, and after that I went out on my own. When I wasn't building boats or raising a family, I was lost in the world of reading about boats, boatbuilding, and history.

Along the way I was asked to teach weeklong traditional boatbuilding classes at the Chesapeake Bay Maritime Museum in St. Michaels, Maryland. I was impressed with the enthusiasm and talent of the many people who took the classes. I resurrected the Challenge Program working with adjudicated youth and building "six-hour" canoes at the *Kalmar Nyckel* Shipyard in Wilmington, Delaware. I saw that building and rowing a boat was a hands-on process that could captivate the imagination and ignite a spark in even the most streetwise youth. I began doing more and more restoration work on older vessels, including Chesapeake Bay working craft. A trip in the Netherlands led me to Lelystad, where one person's dream and the courage to begin ultimately created a ship. Here, a reconstruction of the merchantman *Batavia* had been built by apprentices, students, and volunteers, and throughout its construction the public had been invited to come and view the process. And come they did.

While in Amsterdam I bought *Colonial Schooners* by Harold M. Hahn. *Sultana* was one of several ships that Hahn wrote

about in depth. She had long been one of my favorite small ships and many times I had reviewed the drawings of her done by Howard I. Chapelle, naval historian and one-time curator of transportation at the Smithsonian Institution.

And so, simmering over several years, the above experiences led me to the idea of building a well-documented historic ship of manageable size in the town of Chestertown, with the help of schoolchildren, apprentices, volunteers, and adult students. The shipyard, I thought, should be in town and accessible to all who came to watch and learn. The building of the ship would be an opportunity for education and the construction time would be extended to allow as many people as possible to be touched by the process, to come to know the ship as theirs no matter what their degree of involvement. Just coming to the yard would create involvement.

But who to help make this happen?

Shortly after that trip to the Netherlands, I was rebuilding *Elsworth*, a skipjack built in 1901 and owned by Echo Hill Outdoor School, an environmental education organization based in Worton on Maryland's Eastern Shore. Through this project, I was introduced to Drew McMullen, who had applied to the state's historic preservation trust for the grant that allowed *Elsworth* to be restored. Drew has a college degree that had taken him to Wall Street for a few years before he returned to the camp of his younger days to work at Echo Hill. While there he put to use his 50-ton captain's license, environmental knowledge, love of history, teaching acumen, writing ability, computer proficiency, business sense, and boat-carpentry skills. Our mutual interest in boats, history, youth, and education prompted long discussions while scoping out rot, pulling planks, or replacing the keel, keelson, stern, and decking.

It wasn't long before I shared with him the idea of building *Sultana* in Chestertown. *Sultana*'s history meshed with the colonial character of Chestertown, her size was affordable and scaled to the Chester River, and she was well documented and beautiful. And so, as Drew describes, we teamed up and presented the *Sultana* project to the incredibly receptive and enthusiastic Chester River Craft and Art, Inc. Drew became the project director, working for the organization; Swain BoatBuilders, L.L.C., became the contractor to build the vessel using shipwrights (selected for teaching ability as well as carpentry skill), volunteers, students, and apprentices. Drew coordinated the programming for the classes of local schoolchildren we worked with, and all of us offered free tours to anyone who showed up. And, as with *Batavia,* show up they did.

Because of Drew's incredible commitment and his multitude of exceptional skills, the schooner *Sultana,* in less than four years, went from "You're gonna do *what? Where?* By *when?*" to national recognition as a model for building a historic ship reproduction—with community involvement, on time, and under budget. Drew was the site superintendent, requisition master, educator and coordinator, writer, historian, buffer, budget minder, lunchtime grill meister, sign maker, safety engineer, "gofer," complaint mediator, fundraiser, detailer, town/county/ Coast Guard intermediary and regulatory expert—the list is never-ending. Working with Drew, with his attention to detail and historic accuracy, gave all of us the assurance that the schooner *Sultana* would be nothing short of perfection in both her building and, upon completion, her mission as the schoolship of the Chesapeake Bay.

A person can have a dream, but bringing it to life is certainly easier when others also believe in it. I feel honored and privileged that Drew McMullen shared my vision, put it to paper, and was instrumental in bringing it to life. And just as capably, he puts the building experience to paper, weaving the history of the *Sultana* of 1768 with the story of the *Sultana* of 2001 and recognizing all the people who helped the dream become a reality.

May you also share in this experience.

—John E. Swain

# Preface

A rare combination of people, events, and resources, the schooner *Sultana* project created a legacy for the Chesapeake Bay. Children, tourists, residents, and history buffs will reap the benefit from the efforts of those who built *Sultana:* John Swain, whose vision and craftsmanship guided the project; Drew McMullen, whose careful management made the project work; Michael Thielke, whose persuasive ability convinced the Chestertown community to invest in the past and in the future; and Joyce Huber Smith, who embraced the vision with her commitment and funds. Most of the labor required to construct *Sultana* came from volunteers. Many people made major commitments in time and money to build this lovely ship.

During *Sultana*'s construction, there was no limit to the number of visitors who had access to the construction site. All were treated to a complete tour of the shipyard by the working staff. Classes from local schools were frequently visible as the children learned various woodworking techniques. Classes in ship construction were conducted for many age groups. For two and a half years, the shipwrights and the volunteers labored, and finally, in a grand celebration, the ship was launched by a huge derrick that lifted her from the streets of Chestertown and placed her into the Chester River.

The March 2001 launch started a new history for a new *Sultana,* as a classroom and as an ambassador for Chestertown, Maryland. *Sultana* is not a large vessel. Her original role in the Chesapeake was not momentous. But the new *Sultana* will help young people understand the past better; they will learn how twenty-five crewmen lived on the vessel for many months at sea under very primitive conditions. They will marvel at the skill of the Boston craftsmen who created her and at the abilities of the current day craftsmen who so ably reconstructed her.

For the documentation of *Sultana*'s construction, I used Leica R cameras with Leica lenses from 35mm to 100mm, so as to minimize distortion. Mostly I used Agfachrome 100, a very neutral film. Kodachrome and Ektachrome were used occasionally, usually for speed. I used natural light with few exceptions, and no filters. A shoulder mount was used to provide stability.

In documenting the construction and the launch, I was given complete cooperation by the staff. Without this unprecedented access and help from Drew, John, Mike, Jim, Richard, A.J., Josh, and Rafe, this book could not have been completed. I applaud Drew's writing as the story comes alive under his pen. I thank my wife and partner, for in heat, rain, and cold, she was always with me—her attachment to the project was as great as mine. I wish to thank those innumerable volunteers who gave so unselfishly of their money and time to create the classroom ship. Finally I wish to recognize those craftsmen and seamen who over two hundred years ago gave us the start of our story.

—Lucian Niemeyer

If I could have the opportunity to send a single message back in time to *Sultana*'s commander, Lieutenant John Inglis, or to her Master, David Bruce, it would be this: "Write more in your log-books!" Though *Sultana*'s logs are valuable and instructive historical documents, they also tend to leave much to the imagination. Take for instance Lieutenant Inglis's entry of October 23, 1772:

> Hard gales and squally Wr. with rain & a great deal of sea from the WSW board at 2 shipped a Sea filled the boat washed away the Companion & overset the binnacle lay'd the Schooner on her beam ends cut away the boat and let her go overboard to save the schooner She righted brought her to again split the foot of her foresail
>
> John Inglis, Commander
> David Bruce, Master
> William Piddle, Midshipman

Think what Patrick O'Brian could have done with such raw material!

While I am no Patrick O'Brian I have made my best attempt to flesh out several of *Sultana*'s log entries in order to give the reader a sense of what it might have been like to sail on this, the Royal Navy's smallest schooner, in the tumultuous years between 1768 and 1772. The historical descriptions contained in this book, though based upon primary documents and extensive research, should be considered an interpretative account rather than a rigorous academic work.

My efforts in creating the historical passages were aided greatly by the work of several individuals. Paramount among these is Harold M. Hahn, whose book, *The Colonial Schooner: 1763–1775*, first inspired John Swain to consider building *Sultana*. Hahn's detailed cataloging of *Sultana*'s primary documents was a key factor in the ultimate selection of this particular vessel for reconstruction.

It would have been impossible for me to write the passages entitled "July 1768: John Inglis Takes Command" and "July 1770: Inglis Meets George Washington" were it not for the research of Kees de Mooy. In the course of writing his senior thesis at Washington College in Chestertown, Maryland, Kees uncovered the long-hidden biography of *Sultana*'s commander, John Inglis, contained in the 1914 book by John Alexander Inglis, *The Family of Inglis of Anchindiary and Redhall*. Even more impressive was Kees's discovery of Inglis and Bruce's visit with George Washington at Mt. Vernon in July of 1770, an event that was unknown to the most dedicated Washington scholars until Kees made the connection between Washington's journals and *Sultana*'s logbooks. Kees's research and writings on *Sultana* undoubtedly provide the most thorough and complete academic account of the schooner and her crew compiled to date.

My recollection of the events surrounding the modern *Sultana*'s origins and construction was aided greatly by John Swain and Melinda Bookwalter. The contributions of my mother Constance G. McMullen and those of Emily Porter were also essential to the process. Small portions of the modern narrative contained in this book were previously published in the spring 2000 issue of the *Alumni Horae* Magazine of St. Paul's School in Concord, New Hampshire, under the title "Raising the *Sultana*."

Finally, I am indebted to Lucian Niemeyer for conceiving this book and for asking me to contribute to it. Through Lucian's beautiful photographs, the story of Chestertown's *Sultana* will be remembered long after the schooner and those who wrought her have passed from the earth.

—Drew McMullen
In Lieutenant Inglis's cabin on board *Sultana*,
Annapolis Harbor, Saturday, 18 August 2001

# Schooner *Sultana*

*March 23, 2001. The schooner* Sultana *awaits her launch at the foot of High Street in Chestertown, Maryland.*

*Chapter 1*

# 2001: The Dream Becomes a Reality

It is about a half hour past sunset on March 23. I am sitting on a park bench on the shore of the Chester River in the small, normally quiet town of Chestertown, Maryland. I'm simply trying to take it all in. Before me is as beautiful, unlikely, and incredible a scene as I ever expect to see. Tied alongside the small town wharf lies the seemingly misplaced United States Army barge derrick *Keystone State.* She is an enormous, 200-foot-long mass of modern gray steel lit up like a city and crawling with VIPs, guests, and a host of army personnel in camouflage garb. Directly opposite the wharf stand the beautiful colonial homes of Chestertown, their rippled glass windows and stout brick walls reflecting the last glow of the setting sun. Poised between these oddly juxtaposed bedfellows and surrounded by a throng of onlookers sits the hub around which this account turns. Her name is *Sultana* and though by appearance she is nothing more than a traditional wooden schooner (albeit a yellow one), for those of us fortunate enough to have participated in her creation she is far more than that—she is nothing short of magic.

At this moment I am quite certain that I have never been so tightly wound in my life. It's as if a giant spring has been slowly coiling itself within my chest for the past four years, building up energy and anticipating the appointed hour when it will be permitted to let loose. That hour has almost arrived. If all goes well, at 10 o'clock tomorrow morning *Keystone State* will hoist *Sultana's* 55 tons several stories into the air, swing her out over the water, and place her gently into the Chester River. It is a moment I have been working toward and obsessing over since my friend, master boatbuilder John Swain, first approached me with the concept of building *Sultana.* It now seems a lifetime ago.

I am not the only one who is anxious this evening. Though I have the distinct pleasure of relating the story of *Sultana* it would be a mistake to assume that this is my story. Nothing could be further from the truth. All around Chestertown, Kent County, and the rest of Maryland's Eastern Shore, scores if not hundreds of people have dedicated themselves to building this little yellow schooner—people who, like me, are bursting with anticipation at the thought of tomorrow's long-awaited event.

One short block up the street from where I sit is the home of Joyce Huber Smith, leader of the organization that has financed and overseen this improbable endeavor and the individual who, as much as anyone, directed her professional and personal commitment toward helping *Sultana* navigate the transition between dream and reality. There is very little question in my mind as to how Joyce will sleep tonight—she won't. The idea of the unblemished *Sultana* soaring through the air as ten thousand people look on (and the remote possibility that *Keystone State* might drop her) is almost more than she can take.

A little bit farther up town is the home of Michael Thielke. It is now almost four years ago that John and I—with big visions in mind and *Sultana*'s plan in hand—arrived unannounced at Michael's door. It is quite possible that had he not shown us in that afternoon and taken the time to consider our unusual idea, the Chestertown waterfront would be a quiet and empty place this evening. As he has been each day for the past four years, Michael right now is undoubtedly busy working the details, making certain that nothing and no one has been forgotten, and that tomorrow morning everything will go perfectly according to plan.

Then of course there is John Swain himself, the shipbuilder, the man who four years ago not only had an inspired—if seemingly farfetched—idea, but also had the self-confidence and persistence to pursue it tirelessly until he saw it realized. How amazing is that, and how unusual! John is at home tonight in a small, wood-heated house tucked beneath a stand of towering poplars at the headwaters of the Chester River. With him are his wife Melinda and family members who have traveled great distances to be with them this evening. I can only imagine the thoughts that must be running through John's head tonight. It must be an awesome feeling to have created something that has added so much joy to the lives of so many people.

This is not a standard boatbuilding story. While the record of *Sultana* is about the building of a schooner it is far more than that: it's a story about people. The individuals who have helped to pull off this small piece of inspired lunacy are the greatest people I have ever known. Though the journey we've taken together has had its share of ups and downs, collectively we have been very blessed. That is why tonight, lurking beneath the anticipation and exhilaration that all of us feel about *Sultana*'s impending launch, there is just a tinge of sadness. A chapter in our lives will come to a close this weekend, and once closed, it can never be reopened.

I guess that's why I'm here tonight, to say good-bye, but also to say hello. By this time tomorrow the *Sultana* we have known for the past four years will be gone. In her place will be a new, untested *Sultana*, taking her first cautious "steps" out onto the water. Though I've tried many times to envision what the coming day will bring and to imagine what adventures *Sultana* might have in store in the years ahead, there's no way to know what the future holds. There is only one thing I can say with absolute certainty about the new *Sultana*: I can hardly wait to meet her.

*Chapter*

*2*

# July 1768: John Inglis Takes Command

No doubt, Lieutenant John Inglis was an excited young man on the morning of July 15, 1768, as he made his way through the Royal Navy Yard in Deptford, England.[1] Inglis was a sailor, and for a sailor of his day there was no place in the world that could compare with the Deptford Yard—the working heart of Britain's Royal Navy.

The Deptford of 1768 was a place of great energy and activity, a giant machine fueled by the work of thousands of sailors, shipwrights, sailmakers, caulkers, rope makers, gunsmiths, and riggers. Walking through the yard Inglis was surrounded by dozens of the Royal Navy's largest and most powerful warships, more than a few of which were destined for famous careers under the command of icons like Nelson and Cook. In every direction work was underway. New masts were being raised and cannons fresh from the foundry were being hoisted onto newly laid decks. The noise of caulking mallets resounded, and the smell of oil and pitch permeated the air.

History was being made that summer in the Deptford Yard, and the men who worked there knew it. The British Empire was on the move. In the previous decade England had soundly defeated her traditional enemies, France and Spain, in the process amassing a global empire that would have been unimaginable to even the most ambitious British imperialists of the previous generation. In no small measure this sprawling and somewhat tenuous empire had been gained through the unprec-

edented dominance of the Royal Navy, and the continuing existence of both the empire and the British nation depended directly upon the future success of that same institution.

The young King George would probably have forgiven John Inglis that morning for not having the fate of the empire as the foremost thought in his mind. At the age of twenty-five Inglis was about to have an experience that has been cherished by officers of all navies before and since—he was en route to inspect his first command, His Majesty's armed schooner *Sultana*. Though still young, Inglis had been preparing for this moment since childhood.

Born in Philadelphia on March 20, 1743, John Inglis was the sixth of eleven children born to John and Catherine Inglis. Almost from birth Inglis was exposed to ships and the sea. Inglis's father, a prominent Philadelphia merchant, owned several small sailing vessels which he used to import ironwork and hardware from the British Isles. It is not difficult to picture the young Inglis and his father frequenting the wharves of colonial Philadelphia, inspecting new cargo as it arrived from England or overseeing the maintenance and repair of the family fleet.[2]

Inglis was apparently a feisty and rambunctious child. Relatively early in his academic career he succeeded in getting expelled from school. The description of Inglis's expulsion as it is related in the Inglis family history can hardly be improved upon:

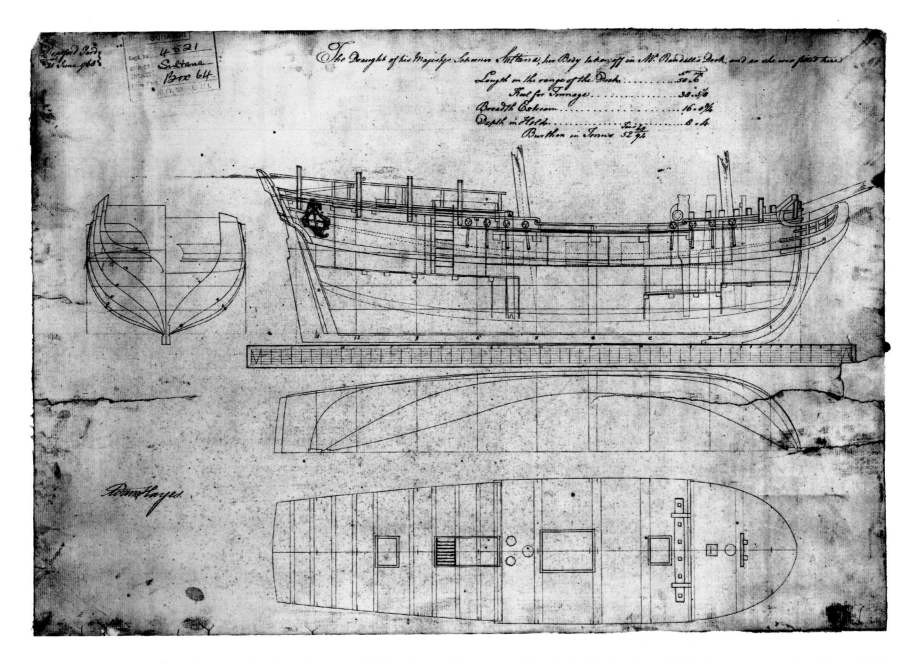

Originally built as a merchant ship in Boston in 1767, the schooner *Sultana* was sailed to England in the winter of 1768 where she was purchased by the British Royal Navy. As part of the purchasing process the Royal Navy made a detailed survey of *Sultana*, shown here. Very few American-built, colonial-era vessels have been recorded in such exacting detail. Courtesy National Maritime Museum, London, negative #4521.

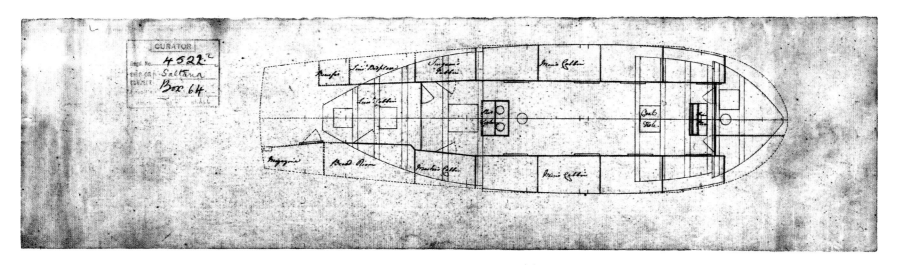

*When the Royal Navy recorded* Sultana *in 1768, surveyors made a detailed rendering of the schooner's belowdecks accommodations. The 1768 accommodations plan was reproduced almost exactly on the new* Sultana. *Courtesy National Maritime Museum, London, negative #4522.*

"He (Inglis) was at feud with his schoolmaster, so he made a dummy figure to represent him, and trained his dog to pull off its wig. After due rehearsal the trick was performed on the schoolmaster, and John Inglis was expelled.[3]"

His formal academic career thus ended, Inglis turned his energies to the sea. In 1757, at the age of fourteen, he joined the crew of HMS *Garland.* Though his tenure with the ship was brief (just two months) and his departure ignoble (he deserted), Inglis was nonetheless taken with life in the navy. He returned to His Majesty's service in 1758 on board HMS *Hussar* and began to work up through the navy ranks, becoming a midshipman in 1759 and earning his lieutenant's certificate in 1761. By 1768, after a decade at sea, the young Inglis was apparently considered an able enough sailor and leader to be given his first navy command.[4]

As Lieutenant John Inglis approached *Sultana* that morning he was under no illusion that she would rank with the greatest ships of the Royal Navy. Established as a revenue schooner, *Sultana* was one of the lowest rated vessels in the British fleet. Even so one could hardly blame Inglis if he was mildly disappointed when he first saw her. Tied alongside the rotting hulk of a decommissioned man-of-war, *Sultana*—stripped of her masts, sails, and rigging—was almost comically small.[5] Measuring just 50 feet 6 inches from stem to stern, the length of her deck could be walked by an average man in only twelve strides! At "52 and 64/92 tons burthen," *Sultana* was almost certainly the smallest active-duty vessel in the entire navy![6]

All that aside, Inglis could identify with certain aspects of this diminutive schooner. Built as a small merchantman, *Sultana* was very similar to the vessels in his father's fleet. Also, like Inglis, *Sultana* was not a product of the British Isles but of America. The keel for the schooner had been laid at Benjamin Hallowell's shipyard in Boston, Massachusetts, during the first half of 1767. Hallowell, one of the colonies' most respected shipbuilders, had been contracted to build *Sultana* by Sir Thomas Asquith, a South Hampton merchant who intended to use her as a combination cargo schooner and yacht.[7]

Upon the schooner's completion in the fall of 1767, Asquith, for reasons that are still unclear (it is theorized that perhaps he was in need of some quick cash), arranged for his close friend, Admiral Edward Hawke, to facilitate the sale of *Sultana* to the Royal Navy. Since the end of the Seven Years War in

1763, the British Parliament had imposed a series of increasingly unpopular taxes on the American colonists in order to pay off the substantial debt amassed during the war and to help support the increased military responsibilities of the enlarged empire. Parliament had given the unpleasant task of enforcing these new taxes to the Royal Navy, who, in turn, created a small fleet of patrol boats or "revenue cruisers," comprised principally of small American-built schooners like *Sultana*. The American schooners fit the Royal Navy's needs to a tee. They were quick, maneuverable, of relatively shallow draft, and, most importantly, cost-effective, both to purchase and to operate.

Inglis's inspection of *Sultana* revealed that there was no shortage of work to be done. Though the vessel had been soundly wrought by her American builders, she was nonetheless in need of a complete refit to make her suitable for navy service. Already, Deptford's riggers were in the process of building a new rig to increase the schooner's speed. The *Sultana* that had arrived in Britain with a relatively slow five-sail merchantman rig would be leaving with a greatly expanded square-topsail rig and a new set of fourteen sails. An order had been placed for eight half-pound swivel guns and a cache of sea-service muskets to give the schooner a bark and bite disproportionate to her tiny size. *Sultana* was also scheduled for a complete overhaul belowdecks. The vessel's open cargo hold would be converted into living quarters suitable for twenty-five men, and a galley and ship's stove would be built to feed them.[8]

Time was critical. Inglis was under orders to depart for action in America as soon as *Sultana* could be readied. For the second time in three years, royal authority in the colonies looked as if it might completely unravel. In 1765–66 the cause of the colonists' discontent with the Crown had been the Stamp Act, which dictated that a tax be paid on all legal documents created in the colonies. Among the colonists, the act prompted a violent response that was completely unexpected by Parliament. There was no solution for it other than to repeal the law. In part their hand had been forced because only a handful of British troops were actually stationed in the thirteen colonies and thus enforcement of the Stamp Act by coercion was not an option.

In the summer of 1767, the king and Parliament resolved to reassert their recently challenged authority over the colonies—especially their authority to tax—and enacted the Townshend Acts or "Tea Taxes." This time if the colonists resisted, Britain was prepared to respond with force. Already reports were filtering in from the colonies describing riots in opposition to the tea taxes. Plans were in the works for the Royal Navy and the British Army to occupy and subdue what was becoming the traditional capital of colonial discontent—Boston.

Inglis had but a few short weeks to prepare *Sultana* not just for the storms of the North Atlantic but also for the more unpredictable political storm that was brewing on the other side of the ocean. Whatever happened in North America, Inglis, *Sultana*, and her crew would have a front row seat for the action.

*Chapter*
*3*

# 1997: The Idea Becomes a Plan

The first time John Swain asked me to help him with *Sultana* I thought he was probably crazy but, even so, his idea was compelling. It was February 1997. At the time I was working as a captain/teacher/fundraiser for Echo Hill Outdoor School, a nonprofit educational organization on Maryland's Eastern Shore that specialized in teaching children about history and the environment. For most of the previous two years John and I had worked side by side to rebuild two historic wooden vessels employed by Echo Hill as floating classrooms—the 1901 oyster-dredging skipjack *Elsworth* and the 1957 oyster buyboat *Annie D.*

## Setting the Stage for *Sultana*

The mid-1990s found John Swain in his third decade as a builder and restorer of wooden boats. Born outside of Dover, Delaware, John had spent most of his life on the Delmarva Peninsula, that peculiar and relatively isolated strip of land bordered on one side by the Atlantic Ocean and on the other by the Chesapeake Bay. In 1966, when John began his apprenticeship as a boatwright at the Applegarth boatyard in Oxford, Maryland, the Delmarva Peninsula—and more specifically the Eastern Shore of Maryland and Virginia—was one of the increasingly rare places in North America where wooden watercraft were still widely built and employed. A visitor to the creeks and marshes of the Eastern Shore in 1966 would have seen thou-

sands of wooden boats of various sizes and descriptions, most dedicated to the harvesting of the Chesapeake Bay's incredible natural bounty of fish, crabs, and oysters.

Thirty years later there were far fewer wooden boats to be found on the shore. Most of those that remained manifested the inevitable deterioration that comes with advanced age and rigorous service. The introduction and acceptance of fiberglass as the primary building material for smaller vessels, coupled with the decline of the Bay's various fisheries due to pollution, development, and overharvesting, had sounded the death knell for the widespread use of wood in boat construction. By the 1990s most of the boatbuilders of John's generation had already made the transition to fiberglass, steel, or other modern modes of construction. Though John had from time to time dabbled in fiberglass through the course of his thirty-year career, he had always returned to wood, eventually becoming one of the Chesapeake's most competent and respected builders of wooden boats.

Time had been much kinder to John than to many of the vessels he had restored over the years—at fifty-five, he still had the frame, strength, and stamina of a man half his age. His bushy red hair had just begun to reveal the occasional strand of white, and his skin, though toughened by work and time, exuded the glow of a man in his prime. Most noticeable though were his eyes, not so much for their color but for what they revealed about the person behind them. John had the eyes of a

*This roughly rigged model of* Sultana *was donated to the* Sultana *project by Thomas McHugh and served as a source of inspiration for the building crew during the early phases of the project.*

man who, though weathered by years of experience, had somehow retained an almost childlike ability to dream—at least that is how I saw him.

When John and I joined forces for the restoration of *Annie D* and *Elsworth*, I was twenty-four and had just started working at Echo Hill Outdoor School after a two-year, postcollege stint with Bankers Trust Company in New York City. Though the New York experience had been great, I knew that for the long run it wasn't for me. There were simply too many people and too much noise. I had always loved the outdoors, especially the water, and at about the time my patience with Manhattan had worn thin, an opportunity came along that was too good to pass up.

As a child I attended summer camp on the Eastern Shore and when I became old enough, I worked as a camp counselor during my summers off from college. I made many friends during those seasons on the shore. Included among these were Andrew and Betsy McCown, both associate directors of Echo Hill Outdoor School. After graduating from college and moving to New York, I continued to visit the Eastern Shore regularly. It was during the course of one of these visits that I casually expressed some of my frustrations with life in New York to Betsy. She suggested, half jokingly, that I leave my job and come to work for Echo Hill. Betsy knew I had my captain's license, which I had obtained almost on a whim several years before, and Echo Hill was looking for an additional captain to help run and maintain their fleet of historic floating classrooms. Though at the time I politely declined her offer, within six months of our conversation I had packed the contents of my apartment on East Sixty-third Street into the back of a Ryder truck and was on my way to Maryland.

John and I met about a year later when it came time to rebuild *Elsworth* and *Annie D*. Echo Hill had made me the project manager for the two restorations and John had been hired as the primary contractor. John and I spent the next two years engrossed in the almost total reconstruction of these two proud, old vessels. As the months of hard work went by, John and I developed a good working relationship. We both came to recognize that our strengths and weaknesses dovetailed almost perfectly—professionally and personally. As we were finishing *Annie D* in the winter of 1997, I was not looking forward to our partnership coming to an end. In the course of my professional life I had been fortunate to work with scores of quality people, but John was special—truly one of a kind.

## The Opening Act

The day John approached me about *Sultana* we were finishing up the restoration of *Annie D* at a boatyard near Tolchester, Maryland. It was a Friday afternoon. We were getting ready to go home after a long day of ripping out the transom. "I have something I want you to take a look at," John said and walked off toward his van. He returned shortly with a cardboard mailing tube and pulled out what looked to be the lines of an old schooner.

"This is *Sultana,* the colonial schooner I told you about." I had a vague memory of John mentioning something about this a few weeks before. "I've always thought she would be a great boat to build and have in Chestertown," John said. "I'm going to see if I can make it happen, but it's going to take a lot of work to get it off the ground. I know you're planning to go back to school in the fall, but if you're interested, I could really use your help."

I was flattered, especially since I knew John was not the sort of person who would approach me lightly. Nonetheless I had some questions, most importantly, who would pay for the boat and what would we do with it when it was built?

"Actually, that's what I'm hoping you can work on. You've had a lot of experience with Echo Hill raising money and teaching students on the water. I was thinking this could be the same sort of thing, just a little bigger."

I thanked him and told him I'd have to mull it over. He gave me a short article on *Sultana* and said we could talk about it more after the weekend. I left Tolchester with the idea of *Sultana* spinning in my head. When I arrived home I sat down and read John's article to learn a little more about the boat that had captured his imagination.

As it turned out *Sultana* had a great history. John couldn't have done a better job in selecting a vessel for reconstruction. Built as a cargo schooner in Boston, *Sultana* had been purchased by the Royal Navy in 1768 and used to enforce the "tea taxes" on the North American coast up to the time of the American

John Swain, master shipwright, had the original idea for building a reproduction of Sultana in Chestertown. Swain was inspired partially by a trip in the early 1990s to the Netherlands, where he visited the construction site of another reproduction sailing ship, Batavia.

Revolution. The thing that really set *Sultana* apart and made her a great candidate for historic reproduction was the fact that the Royal Navy had recorded the vessel, her activities, and her crew in copious detail. Amazingly, all of this information (over two thousand handwritten pages including logbooks, crew lists, and surveys of the vessel) had been preserved and was still on file at the Public Record Office in London.

Great history notwithstanding, *Sultana* was still a risky project. I was set to enroll at East Carolina University in the fall to work on a master's degree in maritime history and nautical archaeology. Initially, the idea of postponing graduate school in order to put my energy into such an uncertain endeavor seemed foolish. As I thought about it more, though, I realized that *Sultana* would probably be as great a learning experience as graduate school, and if there was ever a time for me to take a chance it was now. I was single, unencumbered, and had enough money saved so that I could get by if I worked only part time. I could spend the rest of my hours with John, trying to get *Sultana* off the ground. I pondered the possibilities all weekend but by Monday morning I had made my decision: I wanted in.

*Drew McMullen, writer, captain, and longtime friend of shipwright John Swain, was tapped by Swain to help organize the* Sultana *project. The pair had previously worked together to restore several historic Chesapeake workboats, including the skipjack* Elsworth *and the buyboat* Annie D.

## Planning *Sultana*, Making Friends, and Meeting Michael

From the beginning John and I both knew that building *Sultana* would be only half the battle. The other half would be to keep the boat going once it was finished. I had some experience raising money for Echo Hill, but *Sultana* was going to be a much more difficult proposition. We were starting with almost nothing—no organization, no track record, few connections, and even fewer dollars. We needed some serious help.

If we were to succeed in this uncertain venture, we knew we had to start by doing two things. First we would have to clearly define the purpose of the endeavor and the resources it would require. Then, after outlining our mission and business plan, we would have to go out into the community, talk to anyone who would listen, and try to convince a few people that we weren't entirely crazy.

For the next two months John and I worked on *Annie D* during the day and brainstormed *Sultana* at night. Meeting each evening at a small table in the back of John's house, we managed to put together a preliminary mission statement, timeline, and budget. By the end of April, after the first month of these late-night planning sessions, John and I began to go out and pitch our plan for *Sultana*. Reaction was almost always favorable, but we both knew we needed more than verbal endorsements. We needed to find a group of people who would support us and put their full efforts into making *Sultana* a reality.

The big break came when we met Michael Thielke, a successful entrepreneur who had just sold his business and was taking a few years to catch his breath in Chestertown. Margo Bailey, the mayor of Chestertown, had recommended him to us. "Michael likes to think big. I bet this would be right up his alley," she said.

Unannounced, we went to Michael's house. When he answered the door I did my best to tell him quickly who we were and what we were doing. We must have aroused his curiosity because he invited us in. Initially we hoped that Michael could give us some advice on setting up a nonprofit corporation for *Sultana*. The mayor had told us that he was in the process of getting a similar tax designation for an organization he was helping to start up, Chester River Craft and Art.

At Michael's request John and I spent a few minutes reviewing our vision for *Sultana*. Central to our plan was the concept that *Sultana* would be a focal point for education and community building. The vessel would be built in Chestertown by a mix of professional shipwrights, students, and volunteers. When complete *Sultana* would sail the Chesapeake teaching people about the importance of history and the value of the environment. Though the project would be expensive (about $1 million just to build the boat and substantial financial support for many years thereafter), we made the case that the returns for the community would justify the investment.

Michael sat quietly, taking notes and only occasionally asking a question. When we were finished he went into the kitchen for a cup of coffee, then came back and made a proposal that neither John nor I had expected. "It seems as if you have a good idea. What you really need is to organize and get some funding." We nodded affirmatively. "I don't know how much the mayor told you about the group I'm involved with, Chester

River Craft and Art. Basically we're a nonprofit umbrella organization that was formed with the idea of supporting cultural activities in the community. Right now we are principally concerned with craft and art education but I don't see why *Sultana* couldn't fit within the boundaries of our mission. If you're interested I would be happy to approach our board of directors to see if they would consider taking this on."

From that point, things proceeded amazingly quickly, and within a month we had the group of committed supporters we'd been looking for. By the end of April we had become ambitious enough to set a date for the beginning of construction—June 1998. At the time Chester River Craft and Art had less than $5,000 in the bank.

## A Plan for Raising Money

After recovering from the initial euphoria of deciding to tackle the *Sultana* project, we quickly realized that a mountain of work stood between us and the laying of the schooner's keel. Starting at zero we had less than a year to build the foundations for not one, but three significant undertakings. First, we needed to create a fundraising machine that would produce no less than $35,000 a month for the next three years. Second, we had to lay out a sound business plan for *Sultana* that included an innovative curriculum; this would serve the dual purpose of guiding our endeavor and showing potential funders that we were serious. Finally, we had to plan and build a working shipyard that, in turn, could build a custom 80-ton historical wooden schooner, all from scratch.

Michael took on the first task—fundraising—with a zeal and fearlessness that was almost incredible. Most projects like *Sultana* have no shortage of people who are interested in working on the more romantic aspects of the job. Put out the word that people are needed to help build a historic schooner reproduction and scores of people will reply. Ask for volunteers to raise money—serious money—and the crowd will thin out considerably. Ask for someone interested in taking personal responsibility for raising over $1 million in three years for an organization that barely exists and there may be no one at all to talk to.

*Michael Thielke, an experienced entrepreneur, served as the executive director of Chester River Craft and Art, the nonprofit organization that sponsored and oversaw the* Sultana *project.*

With an entrepreneur's drive (and almost no prior experience) Michael began educating himself about the world of professional fundraising. He began to work creating a campaign plan specifically tailored for *Sultana*, and by the end of summer, the framework of the plan was taking shape. In the end it was dictated as much by necessity as by design.

Michael's work and the input of many advisers all led to the inescapable conclusion that if *Sultana* was ever to be built her construction would have to be funded primarily by private contributions. In the short term there were simply no other options. The rural nature of Maryland's Eastern Shore limited the number of nearby corporations capable of donating serious money. The shore location also meant we would not have the political muscle in the state capital, Annapolis, that would allow us to seek significant state assistance.

Aside from the difficulties that would be involved with raising government and corporate money, we also felt that private funding was the best and most appropriate way to go in light of *Sultana*'s mission. If this was to be the community's boat, then it seemed only proper that the community should support her.

By fall Michael had put together a plan for funding the construction of *Sultana*. It called for the creation of a volunteer "development committee" composed of about twenty community leaders who would be responsible for building an extensive network of private donors to fund 75 percent of *Sultana*'s construction. The remaining 25 percent, according to the plan, would be funded by corporate, foundation, and state grants. Like all battle plans Michael's strategy looked great on paper, but its success was completely dependent upon the efforts and coordination of the team that would execute it—a team that did not yet exist.

## A Plan for Spending Money

While Michael racked his brains to figure out how we would raise the money for building *Sultana*, I set out to establish that there was a sound reason for doing so. The experience of other groups suggested it would be feasible to raise money to build a reproduction of a historic vessel; the difficult part would be to find a way to keep it afloat financially once it was done. John and I were aware of more than a few organizations that had managed to build a beautiful vessel only to watch it rot at the dock for lack of a workable mission and continued funding. Obviously we didn't want this to happen with *Sultana*.

In many ways this was the perfect job for me. By nature I am a worrier (if not a pessimist) so I had no problem considering potential pitfalls for *Sultana*. All I needed to do now was to plan out a way to avoid them. Like Michael I started educating myself. An important part of this education consisted of visiting organizations that had engineered similar projects successfully and had managed to keep them vital and viable once the initial excitement had passed. In two months I put more than five thousand miles on my car and met with over twenty different organizations. While each visit was worthwhile, some were extraordinarily so. A handful of groups were kind enough to share every detail of their operations and experience—these included the organizations that built Baltimore's schooner replica the *Pride of Baltimore II*, the Hudson River sloop *Clearwater*, and Delaware's tall ship *Kalmar Nyckel*. The assistance of those organizations and others like them was invaluable.

As fall settled in I wrapped up my travels and sequestered myself in our newly rented office space, a second-floor loft behind an oriental rug store in Chestertown, to begin piecing together the details of *Sultana*'s educational mission and business plan.

Education was the fun part. Except for my time with Bankers Trust, I had worked with children on the water most of my adult life, and I had no doubt that *Sultana* would be an incredible teaching platform. She was just the right size to take a classroom of students out for a day on the water, and what a day it would be. If a picture is worth a thousand words then surely the chance to experience the real thing should be worth several million! On board *Sultana*, children and adults would have the opportunity to learn about and interact with history and the environment in a way that was impossible in the classroom. Instead of just reading about life in the Chesapeake, students would see, hear, touch, smell, and taste it. Instead of learning about history solely from books, students would be able, in a sense, to live it!

We had no shortage of dreams for using *Sultana* as a classroom, but the ideas for funding these dreams were somewhat harder to come by. The type of operation and program we envisioned was first class and so too would be the price tag. First there was the expense of maintaining a wooden schooner that would require almost year-round attention. Then there would be the cost of paying the captain and crew, hull and liability insurance, administration, and fundraising—the list of expenses was truly daunting.

The most important step in our financial planning for *Sultana*'s future was to discard the wistful notion that the vessel, as a schoolship, would ever be able to cover her own expenses. If we wanted to make *Sultana*'s educational program affordable to the average public school group, we could not charge the true full cost of a program. Once we had a firm grasp of this reality the business plan came together relatively quickly. A $1 million endowment was added to our goal and additional fundraising and revenue generating activities were incorporated into *Sultana*'s future operating budgets. In the long run the endowment and the other funding activities would make the project's path much smoother, but in the short run they compounded the obstacles we faced. Within a few weeks the cost of *Sultana* had more than doubled.

# Chapter 4

# September 1768: *Sultana* Crosses the Atlantic

Monday, September 12, 1768—the heart of hurricane season in the North Atlantic. One could hardly call it an auspicious beginning. Only sixteen days had passed since *Sultana's* crew had completed the schooner's refitting, stowed their provisions, and set sail for America. Now, just 324 leagues out into the Atlantic, the young Lieutenant Inglis and the twenty-four men under his command were already in a fight for their lives.[1]

Trouble had started the previous Thursday, September 8. A calm, rainy morning had rapidly deteriorated into an afternoon of gale-force winds, driving rain, and frequent, violent squalls. The crew, still learning the peculiarities of *Sultana's* rig, had lost a good portion of it when, in the process of reducing sail, the schooner's two thrashing topsails fell into the sea and were instantly torn from the masts. Only years of experience and a good dose of luck had prevented one of the crew from being lost along with them.[2]

Friday was hardly any better. Again a reasonably calm morning developed into a strange, difficult, and foreboding afternoon. The sky was gray with clouds. Frequent squalls separated by periods of calm frustrated the crew, who were called upon by *Sultana's* master, David Bruce, to repeatedly raise and lower the sails. When night fell both Inglis and Bruce had the strong suspicion that further bad weather was in the offing. Inglis ordered the crew to lower the topmasts and yards and to prepare the schooner for a storm.

Again the weather confounded *Sultana's* crew. Dawn broke on Saturday with a hazy sky and moderate seas. The pattern of the two previous days held true, however, and as the morning unfolded, the wind wheeled around from the west to the north and increased to a full gale. The seas built quickly and by noon the five-foot "wooden wall" that separated *Sultana's* main deck from the boiling surface of the North Atlantic was being repeatedly breached by an endless procession of towering wind-driven waves.[3] As often as not when Inglis looked down the length of *Sultana* from his vantage point on the quarterdeck he saw little more than masts, rails, hatch coamings, and deck gear protruding from the swirling water, the schooner itself having temporarily disappeared under the mass of a breaking wave.

That evening and the next day, Sunday, brought only intermittent respite from the fury of the storm, usually just long enough for the crew to man *Sultana's* two hand-driven pumps and attempt to clear the schooner's bilges of the water she was taking on at an alarming rate. Conditions belowdecks were appalling. Four days of rain and more than twenty-four hours of waves breaking over the schooner had made *Sultana's* already cramped and dark crew quarters almost unbearable. Everything was wet—clothing, food, bedding—all of it absolutely drenched. The fifteen-by-twenty-foot crawl space that the crew called home was a confused mess of line, sails, and provisions which the men had to negotiate in almost complete darkness

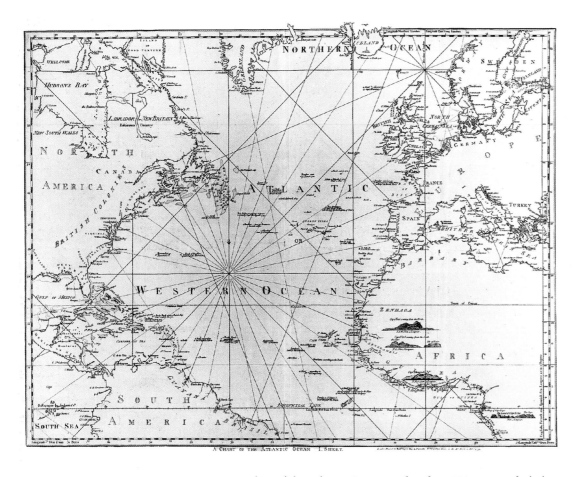

*Sayer's* A Chart of the Atlantic Ocean, *produced in 1775, is typical of, if not significantly more advanced than, the charts that were likely available to* Sultana's *captain, Lieutenant John Inglis, when he commanded the vessel. Courtesy the John Carter Brown Library at Brown University.*

while the schooner heaved and pitched unpredictably. Those crewmembers who were off watch had only the dubious sanctuary of their six-by-three-by-three-foot wooden "coffin bunks" to retreat to. Lying on their backs, soaking wet and hungry, the men could feel the fury of the ocean through the schooner's hull planks and hear the rush of water as wave after wave broke on the schooner's decks overhead.[4]

Topside, the situation was even more terrifying, especially at night. Except when an occasional bolt of lightning flashed an instant of light, Inglis and Bruce were forced to sail *Sultana* almost completely blind, relying upon the direction of the wind and waves to keep their bearings. In the dark even the slightest misstep could result in an immediate and unrecoverable disaster. It was almost a blessing that virtually no one on board knew how to swim. The skill would have only prolonged the unfortunate sailor's agony.

The storm continued to build through the night on Sunday and into the early hours of Monday morning. It had been over a hundred hours—four days—since the crew had managed any significant rest. With each passing hour *Sultana's* situation became more precarious. The constantly immersed deck made pumping the bilges dangerous if not impossible, since the pumps were located on deck. The level of water in *Sultana's* hull had risen steadily since Saturday and the added weight was beginning to take its toll on the schooner's stability. Each time *Sultana* was "knocked down" on her beam, the water in her hold rushed sideways and "up" the side of the temporarily prostrate hull. In order to right herself *Sultana* had to raise both the weight of her rig and the additional weight of the water now trapped inside her hull.

With great concern Inglis had taken note that it was increasingly difficult for *Sultana* to right herself. To add to the problem, the water in the hull was also making it difficult to steer the schooner through the towering seas. As *Sultana* pitched, the momentum created by water rushing fore and aft within her hull was often more powerful than the rudder could overcome. Scrutinizing his men, Inglis could see that the facade of professional concern originally displayed on their faces was beginning to crack, revealing the first glimpses of unrestrained fear. They were losing control of *Sultana* and they knew it.

Inglis's options were limited at best. Without a break in the weather the crew could not pump the hold. If they were to regain control, they had to lower the schooner's center of gravity and stabilize her, but how? The solution that Inglis and his men devised was almost as dangerous as the problem they were trying to solve. Lashed to the sides of *Sultana*'s middle deck were twelve half-hogsheads of beer, containing a good portion of the potable liquid on board the schooner. Each full hogshead weighed nearly 400 pounds and together their weight approached nearly 5,000 pounds. If the crew were to cut loose the hogsheads and cast them overboard they might be able to stabilize the schooner. With this action, though, came great risk. Should the schooner's rig be damaged, or should the rest of their trip to North America take longer than expected, there was a distinct possibility that the crew of *Sultana* would find themselves facing death from dehydration instead of drowning.

For Inglis and *Sultana* a bad option was better than no option at all. The order was given and the hogsheads were quickly cut loose and heaved over the side into the sea.[5] The schooner's sailing qualities immediately improved. Jettisoning the hogsheads not only removed weight from the deck, it also cleared the topsides and allowed water from the breaking waves to drain more quickly over the side. By Monday afternoon the storm moderated and *Sultana* was out of danger. The crew was exhausted but they had performed well. It had been a very close call, the first of many *Sultana* would face under Inglis's command.

*Both* Sultana's *captain John Inglis and her master David Bruce kept detailed daily logs of the schooner's location and activities. Thanks to the diligent record keeping of the Royal Navy and the British Public Record Office, the original logbooks have survived intact to the present day. This particular page contains the entries in Master Bruce's log from June 21 to 26, 1770, when* Sultana *was patrolling the middle and lower Chesapeake Bay. Courtesy Public Record Office, London. Ref. ADM 52/145(4).*

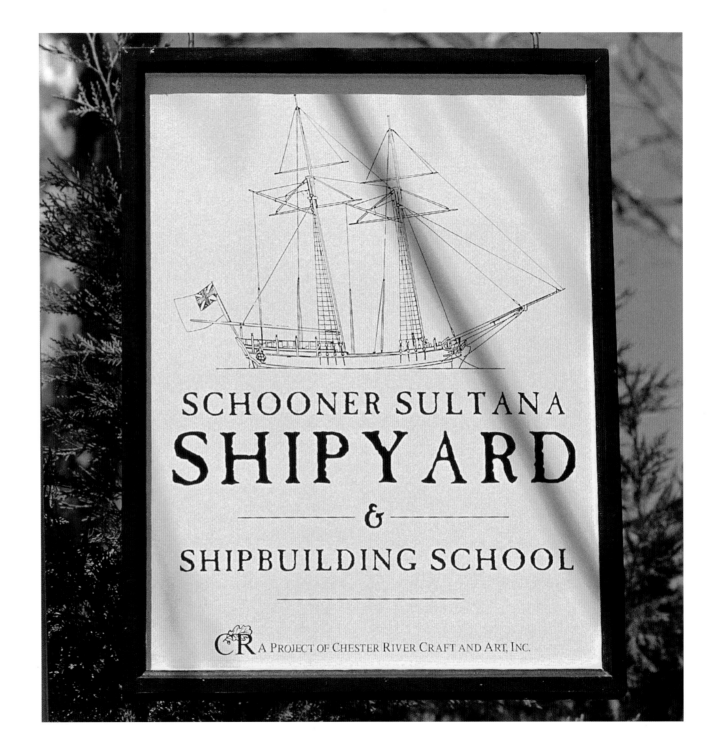

SCHOONER SULTANA
SHIPYARD
&
SHIPBUILDING SCHOOL

CR A PROJECT OF CHESTER RIVER CRAFT AND ART, INC.

# Chapter 5

# 1998: A Community Captures the Spirit

As Michael and I directed our efforts toward building the framework of the business, organizational, and fundraising plans, John worked to tie up the loose ends of his own business so he could turn his attention full-time to *Sultana*. By the fall of 1997, with John's slate cleared, we were able to begin planning in earnest for the construction phase of the project. The tasks ahead included selecting a naval architect; outlining the basic construction parameters and the construction budget for the schooner; locating a site and identifying the infrastructure requirements for a shipyard; working with the United States Coast Guard in order to ensure compliance with the innumerable regulatory issues involved in building a historic reproduction sailing vessel; and finally lining up the materials, principally the wood, that would be needed for *Sultana*'s construction.

Today most shipwrights undertaking a boatbuilding project like *Sultana* don't even bother looking for lumber in North America. Supplies of most of the suitable domestic hardwoods—white oak, elm, live oak, and so on—have been decimated by overharvesting or disease. Most contemporary wooden ship builders are forced to search for timber in the dense forests of

Central and South America, Africa, or Asia, which can still yield large, durable, rot-resistant hardwoods.

John wasn't keen on the idea of traveling to Brazil, Belize, or Guyana to get the wood for *Sultana*. Partly this was due to environmental and labor concerns, but mostly it was because he wanted *Sultana* to be as homegrown as possible. His theory was that if most of the wood could be obtained locally, the community would feel a greater sense of ownership over the vessel. Appropriately enough, John found a creative, if somewhat labor-intensive, solution to our timber needs only a couple of miles away from the yard where we were working on *Annie D.*

One morning in early fall, I was working at my computer when John came to find me. "Do you have time to take a quick drive?" he asked. "I want to show you something." I left my keyboard, got into John's van, and off we went.

"I think I might have found the answer to our lumber problem," he said as we drove down the road.

"I'm listening," I said.

"Just wait a minute and I'll show you." A mile or so farther John took one hand off the steering wheel and pointed out the window. "I think it might be right over there." At first I did not have the slightest idea what he was talking about. I looked in the direction he was pointing and all I saw were acres of recently harvested cornfields. I scoured the landscape searching for a barn or any other structure that might be hiding an

Facing page: *The* Sultana *Shipyard sign, which greeted visitors at the gates of the yard, was the first concrete indication that something unusual was afoot at the corner of Cannon and Mill Streets in Chestertown.*

*Sultana's massive ribs were hewn directly from standing hedgerows of Osage orange trees. Over 250 trees were donated and harvested from six separate farms in Kent, Queen Anne's, and Cecil Counties in Maryland. Osage was selected in part because of its strength and resistance to decay.*

enormous pile of planks and timbers. John could tell I was lost and helped me out. "Look at the hedgerow."

It's surprising how something as huge as a hedgerow can be completely invisible if you're not looking for it. There in front of me appeared two rows of huge trees separating two cornfields. I had probably driven past these trees five hundred times but never once had I given them a second thought. "I think that might be the boat," John said, "right there in those trees."

John stopped the van so we could get out and take a closer look. Walking into the hedgerow and looking skyward I knew at once that I had never seen trees like these before. Sprawled out above my head were the most bizarrely contorted tree limbs imaginable. Some of the branches bowed through a full ninety-degree arc and then proceeded to reverse the bend again, forming a giant wooden sine curve. Because of the close proximity of the trees, the branches of one tree were often tightly woven through the branches of its neighbor, creating a scene that resembled a line of towering trees standing in the middle of a field holding hands.

"This is Osage orange," John told me. "I was reading a book about ship timber the other week and there was an illustration that showed how the different curved pieces of a tree were cut and used to make the curved frames and knees of ships. It looked just like this hedgerow. We'll have to do some research, but from what I know of Osage it's strong, rot-resistant, and hard as hell."

"Have you ever heard of anyone building a boat out of Osage before?" I asked.

"No," John answered. "But that doesn't mean it can't be done."

## Harvesting the Osage

John was right in his estimation of the qualities of Osage—a month of research led us to conclude that the wood would be ideal for use as framing in *Sultana*. It is one of the most dense, hard, and rot-resistant woods found in North America, comparable in quality, if not size, to the finest tropical hardwoods. Although it was not historically used as a shipbuilding wood this was due mainly to the fact that it was native to a small area of

Arkansas, Oklahoma, and Texas and had only been introduced widely on the East Coast in the mid to late 1800s.

Harvesting and milling trees to obtain the wood for *Sultana* was not something we had originally envisioned. Certainly it had its advantages, not the least of which was that, discounting labor, the Osage was free for the taking, thanks to John's extensive contacts with local landowners, several of whom allowed us to lumber on their properties at no charge. The primary advantage of Osage, though, was that if we selected and harvested the trees ourselves, we could isolate specific trunks and branches that had the exact curves and arcs we wanted for the frames of *Sultana.*

By our calculations we needed approximately 20,000 usable board feet of Osage to frame *Sultana* (a board foot measures 12 inches by 12 inches by 1 inch). This worked out to roughly 250 medium-sized trees. At the time we had two people and one chain saw.

What this meant, of course, was that we needed to develop a dedicated corps of volunteers who would help us harvest the trees, preferably people with their own chain saws, tractors, and flatbed trucks. Hoping to begin harvesting as soon as the sap had gone down in the early winter, we began to look for anybody who could help us.

To our surprise within a few weeks we had a small army willing to march with us out into the hedgerows and do battle. Mostly the group was composed of retired professionals, farmers, and people in search of limitless quantities of firewood. The equipment we needed, namely tractors and trucks, was also surprisingly forthcoming, usually from the farm where we were harvesting. By the first week of December we were ready to get to work.

I'm still amazed at what we accomplished that winter. I think it was possible only because of the initial excitement everyone felt at the prospect of building the boat. Week after week the harvesting went on though the Osage resisted mightily. Not only did each tree have to be cut, each tree also had to be separated from its neighbors, ripped out of the hedgerow with a tractor, and then "cleaned and butchered."

Cutting down the trees was the most interesting and the most dangerous part of the operation. Since the trees were in-

tertwined it was often difficult to predict the direction a trunk would fall when it separated from the stump. There was always the possibility that the base of the trunk could snap off and shoot forcefully in any direction—including straight at the person cutting. Needless to say, a 5,000-pound trunk of Osage striking a person's head or chest could do a frightening and potentially fatal amount of damage. After a few close calls all of us learned to hold the chain saw with our arms fully outstretched (to place us as far away from the tree as possible) and with a clear route of escape already planned out.

Thorns were also an unbelievable problem. Historically this is somewhat ironic since it was the nasty thorn of the Osage that had prompted farmers to plant the trees originally. One of the principal uses of Osage had been as a hedgerow tree to separate livestock. An advertisement from the 1800s claimed that in four years, an Osage hedgerow could grow "horse high, hog tight and bull strong!" I'm sure this was no exaggeration because for those first few weeks (until we learned to dress in several layers of thick canvas clothing and wear protective helmets and masks) the Osage literally tore us to pieces.

Although we couldn't know it at the time many of the people who were helping us harvest the Osage would form the core of the volunteer crew for the building of *Sultana.* Included in this group were two extraordinary people, Donald Hewes and Stig Torstenson, who would become virtual unpaid employees with *Sultana.* Also out in the hedgerows was our friend, notable maritime artist Marc Castelli. Marc was setting out on his own journey to document and record in pen-and-ink and paint every facet of the construction of *Sultana.* Donald, Stig, and Marc would eventually be joined by scores of other volunteers of all ages and backgrounds. Together they would contribute over 70 percent of the manhours required to build *Sultana.*

## A Leap of Faith

By the middle of February 1998 John and our then-weary crew had cut almost all of the Osage we would need for *Sultana.* As the harvesting progressed and our corps of volunteers grew larger I was able to get out of the field and back into the office

*Joyce Huber Smith served as president of Chester River Craft and Art during the construction of Sultana. She was one of the project's most dedicated and vocal supporters.*

ning we were asking these people to be the first ones over the wall with no guarantee that anyone else would follow. What we needed was a brave individual willing to make a large financial commitment with no assurance that the entire project wouldn't go belly-up within the year. Ultimately we were to find this person within our own ranks.

Shortly after meeting Michael, John and I made our first presentation to the board of directors of Chester River Craft and Art. We could tell immediately that of all the people sitting in the room one particular individual, Joyce Huber Smith, seemed most taken with the idea for *Sultana*. Joyce was a trustee of Washington College in Chestertown and over the years had been involved in several significant community efforts both in Washington, D.C., and on the Eastern Shore. As we got to know Joyce better, John and I were struck by her almost limitless energy, enthusiasm, and optimism. At times in the beginning of the project when questions arose as to our ability to pull *Sultana* off successfully, Joyce was always there with an unwavering voice of support.

As the months passed Joyce's involvement with and commitment to the project grew until eventually she too started to eat and sleep *Sultana*. By early 1998 Joyce took on the mantle of development chairperson for *Sultana* and eventually board president for all of Chester River Craft and Art. In her role as development chairperson, Joyce began to work with Michael and other members of the board to build the network of private support envisioned in our fundraising plan. Suffice it to say that no one has ever accused Joyce of being shy. Over the years she had built up an incredible group of friends and acquaintances, and she now began to call upon them to help support *Sultana*.

Joyce was fully aware of the fundraising mountain that loomed before us in the few months remaining before our stated date for the start of construction. Joyce also knew that if we were going to climb that mountain successfully, we would need a strong leader who was willing to set an example for others to follow. I don't know what ultimately prompted Joyce to make her decision but I remember when she first announced it. To a person, we were floored. In an understated manner at the beginning of a development meeting Joyce informed us that she

where I could work with Michael on other pressing needs, mainly raising money and finding a construction site.

The fall and winter of 1997–98 had seen our first successes on the fundraising front. In October we had held our kickoff fundraiser, netting over $40,000. While this was a good start it was peanuts compared to what we would need in the coming months and years. Our construction budget, now greatly refined, required that we have at least $100,000 on hand to get through the first six months of construction. If we were serious about our schedule to begin work in June of 1998 we needed funding—a lot of it—and we needed it quickly.

Because Chester River Craft and Art was brand-new and had almost no assets, our options for raising funds were greatly restricted. At this point in our organizational life no foundation or governmental entity would consider investing in such a new and potentially risky endeavor. Michael and the board had been working diligently to compile a list of prospective private donors, but to date none of the prospects we had approached had been willing to make the leap. In truth, I couldn't blame them. No matter how good our concept and how thorough our plan-would personally underwrite the first six months of construction and contribute a similar amount of money each year until *Sultana* was complete. She was willing to make the first leap of faith, she told us. It was up to us to help her find others who would follow.

## Breaking Ground

For the first time, we were really in business. We had a plan, we had most of the materials, and we had enough funding to get started. The last piece of the puzzle fell into place when the town of Chestertown agreed to lease us a dirt parking lot at the corner of Cannon and Mill Streets as the site for our shipyard. Tucked away in a quiet residential neighborhood the lot was still close enough to the heart of town that it would allow easy access to anyone who wanted to watch the entire construction process. The fact that the site was three blocks away from the water seemed, at the time, only a minor inconvenience, one we were confident could be overcome if we were fortunate enough to be able to think about a launch.

John and I now began working like fiends. It was March. By the end of the summer we needed to lay out, build, and equip a fully functional shipyard; work with the naval architect to develop and refine *Sultana*'s design; put together a professional team of shipwrights and educators; work out the details of the educational programs that would coincide with the construction of the vessel; and, of course, continue to help Michael and Joyce with the quest for additional funding so we wouldn't go broke in September. It was at about this time that the concept of "weekend" pretty much disappeared from our lives.

Groundbreaking on the shipyard took place in June. Although we had interviewed and hired two professional shipwrights, neither would start work until early fall. Most of the labor required to build the shipyard would have to be provided through the generosity of volunteers. To lead these volunteers we were lucky to have Troy Mishaw and Doug Argo, a pair of local builders who offered to oversee the construction of the shipyard's workshop. Also involved was our first group of eight students, boys from Kent Youth, a nearby residential center for adjudicated adolescents. These boys were the first of literally

*The working heart of the shipyard was the Swain and McMullen Boat Shop, so named at the request of Rosalind Havemeyer, one of the project's most dedicated supporters.*

thousands of students who would eventually come to work and to learn at the *Sultana* shipyard.

As the summer proceeded into August the first functional parts of the shipyard rose from the ground. At about this time the people of Chestertown began to take notice of the activity at the corner of Cannon and Mill Streets. Casual passersby would often ask what we were working on, thinking perhaps it was a house or an addition to the town's nearby workshop. To say people were surprised when we informed them we were building a shipyard, and that furthermore we intended to also build a reproduction of an eighteenth-century schooner, would be an understatement.

As word of our plan and progress spread through town a growing stream of people went out of their way to walk up Cannon Street to see if the rumors they heard about a shipyard were true. Among these early visitors were two individuals who ended up staying far longer and doing much more work than I'm sure anyone could have foreseen.

In the early part of August I received a phone call from Lorraine Whitehair, who had recently retired with her husband to Chestertown. She informed me that her seven-year-old granddaughter Alexandra had heard about *Sultana* and very much

"How long will *Sultana* be? Where was the original *Sultana* built? When was she built? What sort of wood will you use to build *Sultana?* How long will it take?" It took the best part of a half-hour to answer her questions, at least those that I could answer.

Aly's final query was to ask if she could help with the building of *Sultana.* Though at the time John and I weren't exactly sure where she would fit in, we knew we could not refuse her request. Two weeks later Aly and Lorraine arrived bright and early at the shipyard ready for the first of what would become countless days of work spanning the next three years. Aly, with her bright pink hard hat, and Lorraine, who displayed an incredible willingness to tackle even the least glamorous of jobs, quickly became good friends with the rest of the volunteers and veritable fixtures at the shipyard.

By the end of the summer we were roughly on schedule. Together the volunteers, including the Kent Youth boys, had built a beautiful 2,000-square-foot workshop. In early September the first equipment began to roll in. Table saws, planers, band saws, forklifts, jointers, adzes, clamps, drill bits, and other tools of every size, shape, and description soon filled the yard and workshop. We were finally ready for the shipwrights.

## Lofting and Other Final Preparations

All summer John and I had been looking forward to September and the arrival of the two shipwrights. While the volunteers had been fantastic, working with a different mix of people every day could be exhausting. We hoped that the addition of the shipwrights would add an element of continuity at the shipyard. We were also looking forward to making some new friends.

Josh Herman was the first to arrive, just after Labor Day. Richard Emory came on board a month later. In their mid-twenties, both men were recent graduates of boatbuilding schools: Josh from the Apprenticeshop in Rockland, Maine, and Richard from the Northwest School of Wooden Boat Building in Washington State. Both had disrupted their lives and moved hundreds of miles to a small town on the Eastern Shore of Maryland to work exceedingly hard for very little money.

*Two cast-iron bathtubs were used to melt the 11,500 pounds of lead that was required to cast* Sultana's *"ballast shoe." Attached to the base of the schooner's keel, the ballast shoe was a change to the original design, added in order to lower the center of gravity of the vessel, thus making it more stable.*

wanted to see the shipyard. Alexandra, or Aly for short, lived with her family in Westminster, Maryland. I arranged for the pair to come by the following weekend when Aly would be visiting.

When Aly walked into the yard I knew instantly that she was not a typical seven-year-old. It was obvious that she was extremely bright but what really caught my attention was how well prepared and businesslike she was. She carried a notebook in which were listed several pages of *Sultana*-related questions.

The first project for Josh and Richard would be to do a full-scale lofting of *Sultana*—the final step in the planning process before the laying of the keel, and the road map for all work for the next two years. Lofting is the process of precisely drawing out all of the lines of the boat (full size) and transferring them to the individual timbers used to build the boat. It is an extremely exacting task that requires intense concentration and allows no tolerance for mistakes. The boatbuilding world is rife with horror stories of lofting errors that resulted in horrendous construction problems and cost overruns.

It took some time for John, Josh, and Richard to interpret the old English drawings of *Sultana.* They were aided in this task by the work of naval architects Jay Benford and Tom Fake of the Benford Design Group in St. Michaels, who had worked hard to clarify the information we had obtained in London. The greatest aid to the lofting process turned out to be the work of the notable maritime historian, Howard I. Chapelle, who had done a great rendering of *Sultana* in the 1930s. Starting with a completely white surface measuring 20 feet by 30 feet (the floor space of the loft) Josh and Richard began the agonizingly slow task of drawing out the schooner one line at a time.

It was almost a month before any portion of the schooner was recognizable. The complexity of the drawing was compounded by the fact that the 30-foot length of the floor was far too small to draw out the full length of the schooner's hull, which was closer to 60 feet. To overcome this spatial limitation Josh and Richard were forced to divide the drawing in half; the forward half of the hull would be drawn directly on top of the aft half. If this wasn't complicated enough, two views of the ship had to be drawn in the same space, a profile and a plan (bird's eye) view, both of which had to be done in the same split manner. Eventually the allotted floor space would have no fewer than eight drawings laid out one on top of the other.

*Shipwrights Richard Emory,* left, *and Josh Herman use a traditional wooden batten and lead "ducks" to lay out and draw one of* Sultana's *frames on the lofting floor. Richard and Josh labored for over a month lofting, or drawing out, a full-scale blueprint for* Sultana.

*Chapter 6*

# October 1768: *Sultana* Patrols Boston Harbor

Fifty-eight days after setting out from England, *Sultana* dropped anchor off St. George's Island in Halifax Harbor, Nova Scotia. It was 8 A.M., Monday, October 24, 1768. Almost immediately upon the schooner's arrival Inglis sent word to the local navy yard that *Sultana* was in need of water. The voyage had taken somewhat longer than expected. *Sultana* had spent the entire month of October within 100 leagues of the North Atlantic coastline. The wind, weather, and currents had conspired to keep the schooner and her thirsty crew just out of reach of Nova Scotia for almost thirty days.

By noon 4½ tons of water had been delivered to *Sultana* along with new orders from the Admiralty. Inglis was to make the schooner ready for sea and depart for Boston at the first possible opportunity. No doubt the crew was disappointed. After more than two difficult months on the Atlantic they had been looking forward to some rest and perhaps even a trip ashore. Inglis assembled the men on deck and officially informed them of the orders they had received. For good measure he made a point of reading aloud the Articles of War, reminding the crew of their responsibilities as Royal Navy sailors and refreshing their memories as to the ultimate punishment for desertion—death.[1]

Less than a year had passed since the newly completed *Sultana* had set sail on her maiden voyage from Boston to England. Much had transpired in that short time. The Boston to which *Sultana* had been ordered to return was a different, more dangerous place than the one where she had been built, especially now that she was in the service of the Royal Navy.

Word of the newly enacted Townshend Acts had begun to filter into the colonies toward the end of 1767. Though at first the colonists were unsure what to make of the complicated new taxes, by the spring of 1768 the citizens of Boston were of virtually one mind in their opposition to the new duties and in their commitment to resisting and undermining them in every way possible. Together the city's merchants and mariners made a pact to cease the importation of all taxed items from England and to procure substitutes, generally through smuggling, wherever they could be had.

In June the newly created Board of Customs Commissioners, the official body charged with enforcing and collecting the new taxes, decided that it was time to send the disobedient Bostonians a message. By their order the sloop *Liberty*, property of one of Boston's leading troublemakers, John Hancock, was boarded and seized for suspicion of smuggling. For safekeeping *Liberty* was towed out into the harbor and set at anchor under the ready guns of the imposing HMS *Romney*.

The seizure of *Liberty* failed to produce the result the customs commissioners had hoped for or expected. The instant the officers of the customs board set foot on shore after impounding *Liberty* they were set upon by a riotous mob who promptly seized their long boat, paraded it through the streets of Boston, and then unceremoniously burned it. The commissioners themselves were forced to retreat to the safety of the small British fort in Boston Harbor known as Castle William. From the confines of Castle William the commissioners sent word of their plight to London and awaited a rescue.

Deliverance for the commissioners arrived three months later on September 30 in the form of fifteen Royal Navy warships and two regiments of battle-hardened British "redcoats." This first wave of British ships and troops quickly rescued the commissioners (who orchestrated a display of fireworks to show their appreciation) and secured isolated beachheads of British control within the city. Intent on expanding their area of control, additional British ships streamed into the harbor throughout October and November in anticipation of the arrival of a second wave of troops from England.

The day after their arrival in Halifax, Inglis and his crew hastily stowed an additional 10,000 pounds of ballast in *Sultana*'s hold, unmoored the schooner, and set a course to join the fleet in Boston to assist with the landing of the second wave of troops. Sailing in company with *Sultana* was *St. Lawrence*, another of His Majesty's armed schooners. Together the two small vessels made their way down the coast of what would become Maine, New Hampshire, and Massachusetts, arriving in Boston two weeks later on November 8.[2]

The scene that greeted Inglis and his crew upon their entrance into Boston Harbor was an impressive show of strength. Before them the masts and rigging of the largest fleet of warships ever assembled in North America stretched like a virtual forest from one end of the harbor to the other. Brightly colored pennants flew from every ship in the fleet and small boats and cutters scurried all around, delivering officers and men back and forth to the town. Dropping anchor only a few hundred feet from Boston's long wharf, *Sultana* found herself within hailing distance of His Majesty's warships *Mermaid*, *Glasgow*, *Senegal*, *Bonatta*, and *Beaver*.[3] With just a few words from the fleet's commanding officer, Commodore Hood, the combined firepower of these five ships alone could quickly lay waste the heart of Boston. There was no mistaking the message King George was sending his colonists—disobedience to the Crown would not be tolerated.

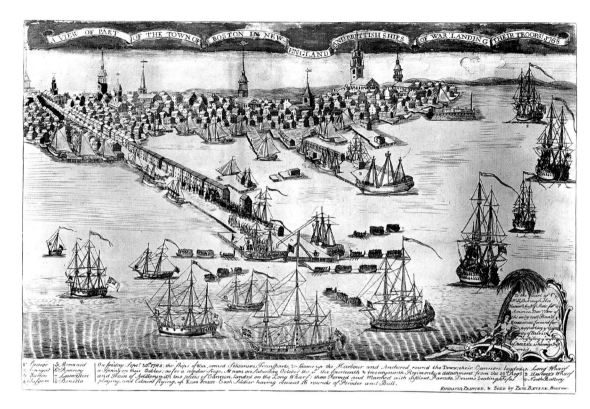

This engraving, made by none other than the famous Boston patriot Paul Revere, shows the British fleet landing the first wave of troops into Boston in the fall of 1768. Though not depicted here, **Sultana** joined this fleet only days after Revere made this engraving. Courtesy Winterthur Museum.

The second wave of troop transports from England appeared on the horizon just two days after *Sultana*'s arrival. Though it took almost a week for the ungainly transport ships to negotiate the difficult entrance to the harbor, by November 15 everything was ready for landing the freshly arrived troops into the city. Early that morning Commodore Hood signaled for Inglis and the rest of the lieutenants in the fleet to assemble on board his flagship *Romney*. Hood informed the lieutenants that the landing would take place the following morning. *Sultana* and the other small support vessels of the fleet were to employ their small boats to ferry the troops in to Boston's long wharf.[4]

Just after dawn the next morning Inglis ordered most of his men into the schooner's two boats and sent them across the harbor to the transports. It was a miserable day with a cold breeze blowing out of the northwest and a steady rain falling from the slate gray sky. The small boats tossed in the water. As they neared the hulking transport ships the men of *Sultana* could see that it had been a hard crossing for these vessels as well as for their "cargo"—the Irishmen of the Sixty-fourth and Sixty-fifth Regiments.[5] The ships' rigs looked as if they had been battered in a protracted battle with the North Atlantic, and the dripping wet, fully laden redcoats, struggling mightily to make their way down the sides of the transports and into the waiting boats, clearly manifested the effects of two months of virtual confinement belowdecks.

It was a short haul for *Sultana*'s troop-laden boats to go to Boston's wharf. Though the weary Irishmen they were carrying longed to set foot on land, they knew that a warm welcome did not await them. A tense and awkward truce had hung over the city since the landing of the first redcoats in Boston one month ago. Though not yet prepared to resist the British Army by force, the Bostonians had made an extraordinary effort to be as uncooperative as possible. Quartering in local homes, barns, and warehouses—a standard tradition within the British Empire—had been denied to the newly arrived troops. The men themselves were mostly poor, underpaid, and badly fed recruits from the slums of England and Ireland. At best, they were ignored by the relatively well-off Bostonians; at worst, they were taunted, threatened, and harassed. This certainly was not a recipe for harmonious relations.

For Edward Cunningham a single day of ferrying troops into Boston's wharf was enough. An Irish seaman from Cork, the twenty-year-old Cunningham likely had little idea what awaited him in the New World when he became the very first to sign on as crew aboard *Sultana* back in July. For someone like Cunningham, born and raised in Ireland under the occupying thumb of the British Crown, the events of that Thursday in Boston were truly revolutionary. These Americans were not like any people he'd ever seen before. Their confidence verged on arrogance, their idealism on naiveté. Still, for Cunningham, there was something captivating about them and the way they saw the world.

Sometime on the afternoon of November 16, 1768, Edward Cunningham made the dangerous decision to desert from *Sultana*. He was the first of Inglis's crew to do so in North America but he would not be the last. Between trips out to the transport ships Cunningham inconspicuously separated himself from the rest of *Sultana*'s crew and quietly merged into the amorphous crowd of Bostonians who were watching the activity. Before anyone was the wiser he made his way quickly up the long wharf into the heart of Boston where, he hoped, a chance at freedom waited for him. At that instant Edward Cunningham became a wanted man—he also became an American.[6]

*Chapter 7*

# 1999: The Schooner Shows Her Lines

By mid-October the volunteers had sunk the pilings and laid the "sleepers," the supporting timbers upon which *Sultana* would be built. The lofting, though not yet complete, had reached a point where construction could begin. John, Stig, and Donald began to hew *Sultana*'s keel from a huge 8,000-pound timber of Eastern Shore white oak. The previous summer John had put out the word to various lumber suppliers that we would need a straight white oak tree, close to 5 feet in diameter and at least 43 feet long, for *Sultana*'s keel timber. Almost exactly one year later, John got a call from the owner of a local lumber mill, Francis Schauber. John and I had worked with him on the restoration of *Elsworth* and *Annie D.* Schauber had just cut a truly gargantuan oak at a farm only ten miles from the shipyard. Upon inspection the timber proved to be ideal. The mill rough-cut the timber and delivered it to the shipyard. By the time John, Stig, and Donald had finished shaping the timber it was 12 inches by 18 inches by 43 feet and weighed only a quarter of its original 4 tons.

## Laying the Keel

October 25, 1998, had been set as the "keel-laying" date for *Sultana*—the day on which construction would officially commence. Joyce, Michael, and a group of volunteers had been working for months to prepare a celebration ceremony com-

mensurate with the significance of the occasion. Among the speakers at the event were Commander Colin Sharp, the British naval attaché to the Pentagon; Commander Gilbert Gibson, chaplain at the U.S. Naval Academy; and the Reverend Martin Townsend, the Episcopal Bishop of Easton. Also participating were the Kent County Community Marching Band and the U.S. Army Fife and Drum Corps from Fort Myer, Virginia. Almost a thousand people, a number roughly equivalent to a quarter of the population of Chestertown, were in attendance as a local Cub Scout troop pulled *Sultana*'s keel over onto the sleepers. Construction had officially begun.

After taking the weekend off, John and the crew returned to the shipyard the following Tuesday. Evidence of the keel-laying festivities was still strewn around the yard but the crowds had gone home, leaving the shipyard crew in peace to begin building *Sultana.* Our plan called for the first twelve months of construction to be dedicated solely to framing the schooner. In traditional wooden boat construction, framing is the process of building the structural skeleton of the vessel, and indeed when complete, the framing looks very much like the skeleton of a large whale. The work John had planned out included shaping the keel (or backbone) of *Sultana*, building the thirty-nine U-shaped hull frames (or ribs) that would define the schooner's shape, building the sternpost at the back of the hull and the stem at the bow, and finally, adding the deck

*Logs of Osage were resawn at the shipyard with the assistance of a portable gas-powered saw. Due to the incredible hardness of the Osage, it was necessary to change the cutting blade on the mill at least once, and often several times, each day.*

beams and other structural pieces that would connect the two sides of the hull.

The sternpost and deadwood (a section of solid timbers spanning the gap between the hull and the top of the keel in the aft end of a schooner) were the first pieces to be added to the keel, and they were to be fashioned of Osage. Though we had spent months harvesting the Osage, working on the sternpost and deadwood was our first experience using it as a construction material. The sternpost was especially difficult to make as it required three 17-foot lengths of perfectly straight Osage. A truly straight Osage tree of any size is a rare occurrence; straight growth is simply not in the nature of the species. Over 3,000 trees were surveyed in order to find the timbers required just for the sternpost.

Due to the crookedness of most of the Osage, and because the shapes and dimensions we were seeking were so specific, John had concluded early on that the milling of the raw logs would have to be done on-site with the use of a portable band saw. The sternpost would present our first opportunity to see how this process, which had sounded reasonable enough in theory, would actually function.

We encountered a few unexpected problems with the Osage. The wood was so hard and silica-rich that it was a nightmare to work with on such a large scale. Saw blades required constant sharpening and the machinery took an awful beating. Also, because the Osage trees had grown in open fields where they were battered by the wind, we found that many of the trunks had large hidden cracks and breaks in them. Often a timber that by every external indication appeared to be perfect proved to be an utter mess on the inside. Eventually hundreds of hours would be wasted on wood that ultimately could not be used.

## Framing

Despite these problems John and the crew persevered and by February 1999 the sternpost and deadwood were fastened into place and the crew could turn its attention to the hull frames or ribs of the schooner. Throughout the winter Josh and Richard had continued their efforts on the loft floor, working to complete the design details that would be required to fabricate the hull

*When the rough trunks of Osage arrived in the shipyard, they were quickly milled into curved, 4-inch-thick slabs, the raw material for framing. The curves in the slabs of Osage were derived from milling the curved trunks and branches of the trees.*

*Design details from the schooner's original 1768 plans were transferred directly to the rough-cut slabs of Osage. This particular piece, which was never used due to defects in the wood, had been designated to be the base or "floor" of one of Sultana's frames. The numerical markings indicate the degree of bevel that needed to be cut into the timber in order to create the sweeping curve of the hull.*

*A side view of a section of Sultana's white oak keel. The keel was cut and milled by Francis Schauber from a Kent County tree. The 90-degree notch cut near the top is known as the planking rabbet and is designed to accept the edge of the lowest hull plank on the schooner. The gray slab affixed to the bottom of the keel is the lead ballast shoe. The shoe has been "let-in" to a notch cut on the bottom side of the keel and fastened with a multitude of silica-bronze carriage bolts.*

frames. The outline of each of the thirty-nine hull frames had been drawn out on the loft floor, including the outside and inside edges of each frame. Additionally Josh and Richard had calculated the planing bevel on the centerline of each frame, marking it every six to twelve inches along the curve. This task alone required well over fifteen hundred individual bevel calculations.

After completing the lofting the next task was to make full-scale patterns for each frame, using thin sheets of plywood. With this done the "fun" work could begin. Pattern in hand, the shipwrights would walk out to the back lot where the Osage was stored. Using a 1958 Massey Ferguson forklift donated by a defunct fish-farming operation, the shipwrights sorted through the towering piles of wood to find that one special trunk or limb whose natural shape perfectly matched the pattern. Though Osage had its drawbacks, its incredible advantage was that just about any shape imaginable (as long as it wasn't straight), was likely to be found somewhere in the tree.

With the Osage timbers cut, the frames themselves were constructed using a traditional technique known as "double-sawn framing." With this technique each frame is constructed of two distinct layers of wood. Since the ultimate goal was to build a frame 8 inches thick, each of the two layers would be 4 inches thick. The individual layers themselves were fabricated from several different pieces of wood known as "futtocks." There were generally four to six futtocks per layer and thus eight to twelve futtocks per frame. The immense strength of double-sawn framing is obtained by staggering the joints between futtocks on the two layers of the frame. In other words wherever there is a joint in one layer a long, unjointed timber is always placed directly opposite on the second layer, in effect serving the same function as a splint on a broken bone.

## Working With the Students

At the rate of one frame per week the construction of *Sultana*'s thirty-nine hull frames would take the project through most of

Facing page: *After the keel laying in October 1998, several months passed before* Sultana's *first Osage frame was raised onto the back of the keel. Eventually the schooner's skeleton would be composed of thirty-nine Osage frames.*

*In the bow and stern of the vessel, where the shape of the hull curves in sharply, the frames of the schooner were constructed in two separate halves (known as "cant" frames), each of which was then fastened into a mortise (chiseled hole) in the keel at a predetermined angle to the centerline. Here shipwright Josh Herman uses a router to cut a mortise for one of* Sultana's *aft cant frames.*

*Master shipwright John Swain guides a slab of Osage into the blade of a hundred-year-old "ship's saw," which was loaned to the shipyard by the family of Jim Richardson, the former owner of the saw and a noted Chesapeake shipwright. According to the family the saw has been in nearly continuous use building boats since the start of the twentieth century.*

Donald and Darby Hewes, both dedicated volunteers at the shipyard, display a traditional eighteenth-century British Royal Navy pennant typical of those that flew on the original Sultana. The pennant was custom sewn by Darby to fly from Sultana's main topmast.

Well over three thousand schoolchildren visited the shipyard to assist with the construction of Sultana. Some students were put to work directly on the schooner while others, such as these children, learned skills like caulking while working on mock-ups created solely for education.

The construction of Sultana's frames moved at the pace of about one frame per week. The Osage frames were notched at their base so they could interlock with the white oak keel. Initially each frame was fastened with two ½-inch bronze rods driven down into the keel. Eventually two ¾-inch diameter bolts were added to strengthen the joint.

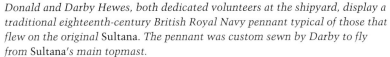

the remainder of 1999. Up to the point where we began the construction of the frames our efforts had been confined almost exclusively to the building of the boat. Though we had worked with students, we had purposely limited their numbers so we could put all of our efforts into getting construction off on the right foot. This was about to change. From the beginning John and I had both thought that the process of building the hull frames offered a great opportunity to teach children about shipbuilding, not to mention math, history, physics, and problem solving. We had every intention of utilizing this teaching opportunity to the fullest extent. Our goal was to see that each of *Sultana*'s frames was either built or raised by a group of students.

As the weather warmed in the spring local school groups became regular visitors as well as temporary workers at the shipyard. Sixth graders learned about simple machines, fourth graders studied colonial history, and third graders investigated the properties of trees and wood. These are just a few examples of the diverse groups that began to use the shipyard as an open-air classroom. When a group of students arrived, work on *Sultana* would cease and each of the shipwrights and volunteers would team up with a small group of visiting students. Each group would get an intimate tour of the shipyard during which they would have a chance to help with various stages of frame construction. At the end of the visit the entire class would divide into two teams and, each using a block and tackle, help to raise a completed hull frame up and onto the back of *Sultana*'s keel.

Building a schooner while working with a steady stream of students was not a simple undertaking. In addition to being an educational challenge it was also a significant scheduling and logistical task. Our timing had to be planned not only for specific days, but for specific hours. School groups usually scheduled their visit weeks if not months in advance, so regardless of any problems we might encounter with weather, broken machinery, or carpentry or lofting mistakes (anyone who says they don't make them is a liar), the shipwrights had to have a frame ready by the time the next school group arrived. On more than a few occasions John, the shipwrights, and the volunteers had to work long into the evening and rise before dawn to complete a frame so as not to disappoint the next group of excited children.

*Juggling the construction of* Sultana *and the involvement of hundreds of volunteers and thousands of schoolchildren was a challenging task. Here several members of the shipyard crew sit down to plan out the schedule.* Left to right: *Stig Torstenson, Richard Emory, John Swain, Drew McMullen, and Josh Herman.*

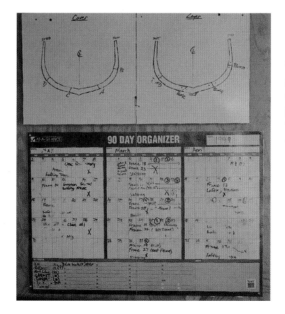

*The construction of* Sultana *was planned in minute detail months, and even years, in advance. This grease-pen chart shows the daily work plan for March, April, and May of 1999.*

I remember one occasion when another boatbuilder happened to be visiting the shipyard during a school program. He was astonished to see the shipwrights and volunteers put down their tools and give their full and undivided attention to the students. "How can you do that?" he asked. "It must slow you down tremendously."

"Yes, it slows us down," John responded, "but really what other point is there in building an eighteenth-century sailing ship if people don't get a chance to see and learn from it? We certainly aren't going to carry cargo or enforce taxes with it."

While hundreds and eventually thousands of students visited and worked at the shipyard, not all of them were children. We had always been confident that there was a sizable population of interested adults who would be eager to get involved with the construction of a traditional schooner, even if just for a short time. As part of our construction plan we had set aside eight weeks in 1999 and 2000 specifically to offer classes in traditional shipbuilding for adults. To our delight after placing a few ads in *WoodenBoat* magazine our classes quickly began to fill with people from all over the country.

There must be something about wooden boats and wooden boat construction that attracts a really nice group of people. It seemed that each student who came to take a shipbuilding class had at least one truly interesting or unusual facet in his or her background. One class was composed entirely of maritime archaeologists, including the likes of Susan Langley, Maryland's chief underwater archaeologist, and John Broadwater, the principal archaeologist for the famous Civil War ironclad *Monitor*. Other shipbuilding school students included doctors, engineers, and freelance writers, as well as general contractors and plumbers. Though the shipbuilding school presented its own set of challenges to John and the shipwrights, these were often the most enjoyable weeks for the workers at the yard. The same must have been true for the participants, many of whom continued on as some of *Sultana*'s most dedicated volunteers and supporters long after their class was over.

*Facing page: Volunteer Dominic Dragotta walks the length of* Sultana's *keel to oil the schooner's hull frames. The hull frames were coated with a mixture of linseed oil, turpentine, and pine tar on a regular basis in order to protect the wood and retard the drying process.*

*The double-layered construction of* Sultana's *frames can be clearly seen in this photo. The two layers of Osage were fastened together with a combination of 1-inch-diameter Osage trunnels (round wooden nails) and ⅜-inch diameter silica-bronze carriage bolts. A protective layer of black roofing tar was used between the two layers to help prevent decay.*

*During* Sultana's *construction great care was taken to make certain that the vessel conformed precisely to the original 1768 plans drawn out on the loft floor. Each frame was located and centered using a hanging "plumb bob." A careful survey of the vessel after the completion of her framing revealed that frames were within a quarter-inch of the loft-floor drawing.*

Temporary 2-foot wooden cleats were nailed to the frames to help maintain the shape and relative position of the frames as the wood slowly lost moisture. The cleats also served as convenient foot and hand holds, helping the shipyard crew maneuver around the unfinished hull.

This large Osage mallet, built by shipwright Josh Herman, was used extensively during construction to "tap" large framing members into place.

Sultana's frames were locked into place between two enormous longitudinal timbers, the keel below and the keelson above. Here the topside of the frames have been notched and prepared to accept the keelson.

The combination of a plumb bob and centerline was used to make certain that the vessel took shape according to plan. A close examination of the foremost frame reveals the signatures of schoolchildren who helped with construction. By the time the vessel was fully framed over a thousand student signatures graced Sultana's hull.

Though very detailed, the original 1768 plans for Sultana rarely included information on specific joinery methods. One joint that was shown in detail on the original plan was the juncture between the keel and the gripe at the base of the stem. This long, saw-toothed scarf was reproduced just as it was drawn in 1768.

More than a hundred years would pass between the original *Sultana's* launch and the invention of the first primitive diesel engines. For safety and practicality an engine was always part of the plan for the new *Sultana*. Due to the particulars of the schooner's design, the engine was placed into the hull early in the construction process. The engine is a 220-horsepower turbo-diesel John Deere 6068.

*Utility jacks, a modern luxury not available to *Sultana's* original builders, were used extensively to lift and adjust heavy timbers. Here volunteer Bill Trakat employs a jack to adjust the joint between the keel and the gripe.*

*Shipwright Rafe Webber employs a chain fall (chain pulley system) attached to a forward cant frame to help nudge the frame into the appropriate mortise in the keel.*

Though each group of students who visited and worked on *Sultana* was different, all the people ended their work projects in the same way—before leaving the shipyard they signed their names on those pieces of the schooner on which they had worked. By the end of 1999 *Sultana* was a truly amazing sight. Standing massive and erect in full frame she was covered throughout with the signatures of preschoolers, elementary school students, technical school students, adjudicated youth, learning disabled children, gifted and talented students, Boy Scouts, and all the rest of the hundreds of people who had in some way contributed to her construction. It was more than John and I could have envisioned that first cold February day standing under the transom of *Annie D* at Tolchester.

## A Trip to London and a Journey Back in Time

Back in 1997 John and I had obtained copies of *Sultana*'s original draft and her survey letter, both recorded at the Deptford Naval Yard near London in 1768 at the time of *Sultana*'s purchase by the Royal Navy. These relatively detailed documents had provided good information regarding the shape and structure of the original schooner—more than enough to serve as a road map for *Sultana*'s reconstruction. To our great surprise our initial research inquiries to the National Maritime Museum in London, England, also produced an interior plan of which we had been previously unaware. This would allow us to reconstruct *Sultana* with great accuracy both above and below deck.

We knew from previously published academic work on *Sultana* that along with the draft and survey letter the schooner's logbooks, crew lists, and correspondence had all been preserved and were part of the collection of the British Public Record Office (PRO) in Kew, just outside of London. John and I were both curious to look at these documents to learn more about *Sultana*'s history and to see if they might provide additional specifications about the construction and outfitting of the schooner.

Thanks to the Internet we were able to contact a researcher in London who agreed to take a quick look at the logbooks and crew lists and give us an indication of their length, scope, and detail. The researcher also arranged to have small sections of each of these documents copied at the PRO and delivered to us

*The cant frames near* Sultana's *transom had the most extreme curves of any frames in the vessel. The protruding ends of the wooden trunnels that fastened the two layers of the frames were often left projecting from the side of the frame so they could be used as handles when raising the frame into place. Once the frames were erected and fastened the trunnel ends would be sawn off.*

*Shipwright Josh Herman,* left, *and volunteer Bill Trakat spent many hours crawling in sawdust underneath* Sultana *fastening and tightening the hundreds of bronze bolts that secure the schooner's frames to her keel.*

in America. The arrival of these copied portions of the logs and crew lists was a turning point in our thinking about *Sultana*.

Even from the short sections provided by the researcher we learned additional construction details and gained valuable insight into *Sultana*'s crew and history. We felt certain that numerous significant facts and details were likely contained in the remainder of the logbooks. Up to this point John and I had both pictured a reproduction of *Sultana* that would be accurate based upon the original draft and fleshed out using standard naval practices of the period. Now we grasped that we had an opportunity to reconstruct, rig, and outfit *Sultana* based almost entirely upon information from the schooner's own logbooks. We began immediately to make plans to visit London to examine the documents ourselves and return to America with a full set of copies.

Our trip was delayed several times by the growing demands of the shipyard, but we finally set aside a weekend in March 1999 to make a quick three-day trip to England. We wasted no time after landing in London. Within hours we made our way to the Public Record Office where, after filling out numerous forms, providing our passports as collateral, and donning a pair of protective white gloves, we were led into a very secure reading room. *Sultana*'s original logbooks were brought in and placed before us on a table.

It was an eerie yet exhilarating experience. Before the trip to London our historic interest in *Sultana* had been focused almost exclusively on the physical attributes of the vessel. Seeing the original logbooks we were faced for the first time with a much more personal and human view of what had actually transpired on board the schooner. The story of the men who sailed and served on *Sultana* permeated every square millimeter of the logbooks. Things as simple as handwriting or spelling evoked the character traits of men long dead.

In our quick read-through of the logs we were astonished by the remarkable and often harrowing events that were recorded in sometimes frustratingly short bursts of text. It was clear that

*Facing page: The beautiful curving shape of* Sultana's *hull was meticulously calculated and drawn on the loft floor, then sawn into each individual frame as the hull was built. Very little fairing, or carving, of the frames was required after they had been raised onto the keel.*

*Though modern power tools were used extensively on the reproduction* Sultana, *the shipwrights often found that nothing was better than a traditional hand tool. Here shipwright Rafe Webber puts the final touches on a mortise for the butt of a forward cant frame.*

Sultana's *forward cant frames and the beginnings of her massive octagonal oak windlass wait next to the boat shed.*

As construction progressed the number of visitors to the shipyard increased dramatically. Here volunteer Bill Bayne takes a minute off from construction to answer questions.

The bright orange sawdust produced in massive quantities during Sultana's framing became a trademark of the shipyard. Several visitors to the yard collected Osage dust and used it successfully to dye clothing. Historically the olive green bark of Osage was used to dye clothing, including almost every U.S. Army uniform in World War I.

Clamps were one of the most important shipyard tools. Large clamps, suitable for holding the massive framing timbers of the schooner, were particularly difficult to find. Eventually the shipyard acquired an eclectic selection of clamps purchased or loaned from boat shops and museums up and down the East Coast.

*Shipwrights Richard Emory and Rafe Webber use a chain fall to maneuver one of Sultana's forward cant frames into place.*

*An extremely long, custom-made drill bit known as a "boring bar" was used to cut a 2⅝-inch hole through Sultana's stern post for the propeller shaft. A wooden track and carriage was built inside the schooner to precisely guide the drill and bit.*

John Swain and Drew McMullen pause for a moment in front of the boat shed to discuss the construction of **Sultana**'s stem. The scaffolding was erected to assist with the lifting and assembly of the numerous, heavy timbers that form the bow of the schooner.

Under sail, the bow of a traditional wooden sailing vessel can be subjected to enormous stress, thus the framing near the bow is considerably stronger than that found throughout the rest of the hull.

the schooner had come perilously close to being lost in great storms on several occasions. The sails, masts, and rigging had been damaged to a great extent no fewer than four times. *Sultana* had been trapped in ice, becalmed in oppressive heat, and infested with rats and other vermin. At times she was so short on supplies the crew was at risk of virtual starvation, and she was undermanned by almost 50 percent due to desertion. *Sultana* had visited scores of ports in the Americas and had encountered merchant ships coming and going to almost every port on the Atlantic. Her crew had been witness to seminal events and themes in American history. They regularly encountered smugglers, immigrant ships, religious refugees, and slavers, not to mention rebellious colonists who attempted to board, capture, and burn the schooner.

Just as exciting as *Sultana*'s logbooks were the vessel's crew lists, also known as muster books. In the muster books were recorded the name, age, birthplace, and rank of every man who ever served on board *Sultana*—102 in all. Though today the events surrounding the American Revolution are often recounted in oversimplified terms, contrasting the rebellious, liberty-loving colonists with the oppressive British royalists, the names and birthplaces in *Sultana*'s muster books gave indications of a far more complicated and painful story.

In many ways the muster books were reminiscent of a typical American Civil War monument that might be found in any small town on either side of the Mason-Dixon Line, where brothers and cousins who fought against each other are listed on the Union and Confederate sides of the monument. The muster books recorded that a good portion of *Sultana*'s crew had been born in England, Scotland, Ireland, and Wales. It also showed that many had been born in American cities and towns such as Boston, New London, Dover, and New York, all places named for a corresponding town or city back in the British Isles. Many of the names spoke of a common heritage and ancestry. More than a few likely had living relatives on both sides of the Atlantic. It's logical to assume that many if not most of these men had been forced to make difficult decisions regarding loyalty and duty, both public and private.

Another group of *Sultana*'s crew had a cultural heritage that reached across the Atlantic to another continent. These sail-

*The final frame hangs from a chain fall waiting to be lowered into place.*

*Construction began on* Sultana's *thirteen spars almost a year and a half before the schooner's launch. Here the jibboom, forecourse yard, and fore-topsail yard hang partially finished under scaffolding in the boat shed.*

*Besides being quick, in the right hands a chain saw can be a delicate precision tool. Here Rafe Webber carefully wields a chain saw to cut* Sultana's *stem to the proper height.*

*Safety was a constant concern at the shipyard. Hard hats were required equipment whenever timbers were being lifted overhead. No major injuries were recorded in over 150,000 man-hours of work at the yard.*

*Just before the last frame of the hull was fastened into place, the shipyard crew slipped some of the larger timbers required for the deck framing and interior planking into the hull.*

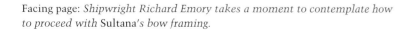

Facing page: *Shipwright Richard Emory takes a moment to contemplate how to proceed with* Sultana's *bow framing.*

Where Sultana's main deck beams join the side of the hull, each is supported by three timbers known as knees. Two of these, called lodging knees (shown in the picture), are fastened horizontally in front of and behind each beam; these prevent the beam from moving fore and aft. A third knee, known as a hanging knee (not shown), is fastened vertically beneath the beam to help support loads on the deck.

Sultana's knees were hewn from the trunks and root systems of hackmatack trees. The species is native to northeastern North America and Sultana's knees were obtained from trees cut in southeastern Maine. Ideally a knee is hewn from a portion of the tree where a branch or root comes off the main trunk at a 90-degree angle. This juncture forms a naturally strong "bracket," ideal for supporting heavy loads.

When the hackmatack knees arrived at the shipyard, they still bore clear indications of their former life in the woods of Maine. These knees resting on the framing platform under Sultana's bow were obtained from the base of a hackmatack tree. The gnarly short arms of the knees are still cloaked in bark from what was the root of the tree. The longer arms, free of bark and relatively straight, were once the base of the trunk.

ors—or their ancestors—had been brought to America from Africa as slaves. No doubt they perceived *Sultana* and the world around her in a profoundly different manner than did the schooner's British-American crew, but they too had faced the problems inherent in choosing sides during the conflict that became the Revolution.

John and I returned from London with a full set of copies of *Sultana*'s logbooks, crew lists, and correspondence. We also had a new understanding of (and appreciation for) the endeavor upon which we had embarked. As we had hoped, the logbooks and muster books greatly expanded our knowledge of *Sultana* and her crew. Upon our return we were fortunate to assemble a trio of researchers who dedicated themselves to delving into the details of *Sultana*'s primary documents. These three were Kees de Mooy, whose undergraduate thesis at Washington College was dedicated to *Sultana*; Susan Haines, a graduate student in history at Washington College who cataloged and examined the schooner's provisioning; and Mark Porter, a graduate student in the maritime history department at East Carolina University who cataloged and compiled the information contained in the muster books. Together these students vastly expanded the academic record on *Sultana* and her crew.

## Deck Framing

Right on schedule, *Sultana*'s last hull frame was raised into place on October 15 by the final shipbuilding school class of the 1999 season. With all the frames in place, work could now begin on installing the deck beams and other structural parts that would support the schooner's deck, such as carlings, hanging knees, and lodging knees. *Sultana*'s original 1768 draft and survey letter both gave extensive information regarding the construction of the deck framing, even including the number and size of the bolts. All the shipwrights were surprised at the incredible strength that had been built into the original deck. Though barely 15 feet across at its widest point, the deck was supported by massive beams measuring almost 10 inches square. Additional strength was gained by locking each beam end into place with three right-angle knee timbers.

Obtaining the proper material for the deck framing was a significant challenge. Again, we wanted to employ Osage for beams

*In order to increase rigidity in the bow of the schooner, a large timber known as a breasthook was fastened to the interior framing directly behind the stem. Here John Swain and volunteer Dominic Dragotta put the final finishes on* Sultana's *Osage breasthook before it is bolted into place.*

*Scores of hours were spent hand-carving the planking rabbet into the stem. Here the 90-degree notch for the rabbet has been carved almost to the base of the stem assembly.*

because of its strength and resistance to rot. However, with the deck we faced the same problem we'd had with the sternpost, namely that Osage rarely grows in a straight line. During the harvesting process we had set aside about twenty-five significant trunks of Osage that we hoped to use for deck beams. This number was just a few more than the actual number of beams called for in the plan. We had always been somewhat apprehensive as to whether we would be able to squeeze the required beams out of this relatively meager pile. Our apprehension only increased as we realized that the casualty rate for the Osage on the mill was higher than we had anticipated.

Every time John lifted a prospective beam onto the band saw we collectively held our breath, hoping that the sawn trunk would reveal a clean, tight piece of wood and not one that was cracked or torn. For a month John worked through the pile and we all kept a close eye on the tally. Finally we were one deck beam short with one remaining timber to cut. Though it would not have been the end of the world if the timber had been a dud, we all dreaded the idea of going back out into the hedgerows. Luckily, the log opened up clean and clear, which we took to be a sign that, despite our struggles, the wood gods were still with us.

The knees for the deck were somewhat easier and far more interesting to procure than the beams had been. Traditionally knees were cut from that portion of a tree where a substantial branch joined the main trunk. A piece of wood cut from such a spot provides a natural 90-degree bracket of tremendous strength. Knees can also be made from the base of a tree where a large root shoots off sharply from the trunk. For *Sultana* John decided upon hackmatack knees. Hackmatack, also known as larch or tamarack, is a reasonably strong and rot-resistant tree common to wetlands and bogs in New England. In order to stabilize itself on wet and unstable terrain, a hackmatack grows roots that shoot out at or near the surface of the ground at regular 90-degree angles to the trunk, thus forming a broad platform for support.

At the time of the original *Sultana*'s construction, there were hundreds if not thousands of men in the thirteen colonies

*In order to stand up to the stresses caused by the sea* Sultana's *bow framing was constructed almost entirely of solid Osage. After the hull was planked, the bow thickness was between 10 and 30 inches of solid wood.*

Extreme care was taken to make sure that modern metal fastenings would be hidden from view in the completed vessel. Where metal fastenings are visible, historically correct fasteners such as these "clinch rings" were fabricated from scratch.

The most refined and complicated portion of **Sultana** was her transom. Shipwright Josh Herman and a handful of volunteers spent over three months lofting and building the transom, seen here under construction from the inside of the hull.

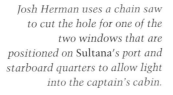

Josh Herman uses a chain saw to cut the hole for one of the two windows that are positioned on **Sultana**'s port and starboard quarters to allow light into the captain's cabin.

Working on **Sultana**'s unfinished deck framing, the shipwrights often resembled early twentieth-century ironworkers walking atop the unfinished skeleton of a skyscraper.

*Before the invention of metal tracks and sail slides, steam-bent wooden hoops were used to secure the leading edge of a sail to the mast. The mast was often greased with oil or tallow to help the hoops slide up and down more easily as the sails were raised and lowered.*

Sultana's *deck beams were fabricated exclusively from Osage. Since Osage trees by nature grow with multiple curves and bends, straight pieces of wood suitable for deck beams were very hard to obtain. Thousands of Osage trees were surveyed in order to find just a few, rare straight trunks.*

56   Schooner *Sultana*

Stig Torstenson, one of **Sultana's** most dedicated volunteer shipwrights, donated over five thousand hours of his time to **Sultana's** construction. Here he prepares the interior of the hull frames to accept the ceiling planks.

Sultana's *major deck beams rested on top of a 4-inch-thick oak plank known as a "clamp," while the minor deck beams were notched into the top of the hackmatack knees.*

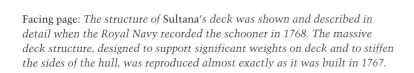

Facing page: *The structure of* **Sultana's** *deck was shown and described in detail when the Royal Navy recorded the schooner in 1768. The massive deck structure, designed to support significant weights on deck and to stiffen the sides of the hull, was reproduced almost exactly as it was built in 1767.*

As the months and years of **Sultana's** *construction passed, the shipyard acquired ever more character with miscellaneous timbers, makeshift buildings, wood scraps, and machinery filling up every corner of the yard.*

The strength of a knee is derived from the curved grain of the wood, which transmits loads from the horizontal deck beams to the vertical side of the hull.

Standing inside Sultana's fully framed hull, a person is immediately impressed by the great volume of space enclosed in this relatively short vessel. Clearly Sultana's original designers were keenly aware that their future profits (or losses) would depend directly upon the carrying capacity of the finished schooner.

Shipwright Richard Emory works with a volunteer to measure the space for a hanging knee. The installation of the hanging knees had to wait until all of the ceiling planking was complete.

*Donald Hewes uses a ball peen hammer and a pin maul to fasten together* Sultana's *deck beams.*

*By the time her framing was complete,* Sultana's *unfinished hull weighed upwards of 75,000 pounds, almost all of it resting upon the schooner's 12-inch-wide keel. In order to stabilize the vessel and prevent her from literally tipping over in a strong breeze, dozens of temporary wooden supports were placed on either side of the hull.*

*Each shipwright and several of the most dedicated volunteers had a set of tools, usually housed in a distinctive, custom-made wooden toolbox. Each worker's personality was inevitably suggested by the design and organization of the toolbox. Here resting below* Sultana's *stem is the box belonging to volunteer Stig Torstenson, as always impeccably organized and ready for action.*

who specialized in providing ship's knees. At the end of the twentieth century there remained only a handful of people in all of North America who carried on the trade. Josh recommended a knee supplier in Maine, Newman B. Gee, and after a little haggling over the price, John and Josh arranged to drive a flatbed trailer north and select approximately sixty knees for *Sultana.*

Newman had been cutting knees for a good part of his life and had amassed a huge stockpile of seasoned timbers that were neatly stacked and tagged in several barns on his property. While John and Josh sorted through the stash, Newman entertained them with an explanation of his unique harvesting technique.

The particular hackmatack trees Newman cut were found in the bogs of southeast Maine. A bog is a unique ecosystem formed when a small stagnant pond is covered over by a layer of leaves and other plant debris until a crust of material, often several feet thick, is built up on top of the water. As the years go by, shrubs and trees take root on the surface of the bog, and they eventually grow to maturity. To harvest the bog-grown hackmatack Newman started by cutting the trunk of the tree about six feet above the surface of the bog. Always careful not to let any wood go to waste, Newman had the trunks hauled to a local mill where they were sawn into boards. With only the stump of the hackmatack remaining, Newman broke out his pride and joy, a six-foot-long chain saw. He plunged the saw like a sword directly down into the bog, then walked in a wide circle around the base of the trunk, cutting all of the roots in the process. Next the stump was pulled out of the bog so Newman could slice cross sections of the stump "freehand" with his chain saw. These cross sections were the raw material from which knees could be fashioned.

After a long day of sorting, John and Josh loaded up the trailer, bid farewell to Newman, and headed south. With the beams and knees in hand the shipyard crew made relatively quick work of the deck framing, completing most of it by the end of 1999. The new year marked the approximate halfway point in the construction of *Sultana,* and for the first time the partially constructed vessel began to take on the feel of a real ship.

*When the deck framing was completed, the strength apparent in its massive structure was truly impressive.*

*Chapter*
*8*

# July 1770: Inglis Meets George Washington

The constantly shifting sandbars at the mouth of the Chesapeake Bay make the sail into Hampton Harbor a challenge for even the most experienced of captains. Though John Inglis was a respected commander who would go on to write a widely read set of sailing directions for the Chesapeake,[1] this time around he had clearly misjudged his vessel's position. It was Saturday morning, July 21, 1770. *Sultana* was hard aground on a shallow sandbar at the entrance to Hampton Harbor, Virginia.[2]

It had been more than a year and a half since *Sultana* had first seen action in Boston. In the intervening months the Admiralty had kept Inglis and his men busy, placing the schooner on station alternately in Rhode Island, New York, and Philadelphia. Though there had been some difficult moments at first, Inglis and his men were now experienced and indeed proficient at accomplishing their primary mission—stopping, "rummaging," and, if necessary, seizing merchant ships suspected of smuggling prohibited goods into or out of British colonial ports in North America. It was a proficiency which, needless to say, went completely unappreciated by the colonists upon whom it was practiced.

Of the men themselves very few, eight to be exact, remained from the original party of twenty-three that had set out from England in the summer of 1768. A select number had left *Sultana* with the blessings of the Royal Navy in order to begin a new life in America. Others, like surgeon's mate John Huxley

and clerk William Dearl, had departed the schooner only in death. Most of *Sultana*'s original crewmembers, however, had followed the lead of Edward Cunningham and run from the schooner without permission. By the summer of 1770 replenishing *Sultana*'s constantly deserting crew from the ranks of the local American population had become a significant challenge for Inglis, made even more difficult by the Boston Massacre which occurred in March of that year.[3]

Under the watch of Master David Bruce the crew spent the morning of July 21 loading the schooner's kedging anchors and grappling hooks into the small boats and rowing them out at various angles to *Sultana*'s grounded and prostrate hull. After securing the anchors to the schooner with long hemp cables, the kedges were lowered overboard where they worked themselves into the rippled, sandy bottom of the Chesapeake. By turns the slack on each cable was taken up by the crew on the schooner's stout oak windlass and *Sultana*—with much protest, groaning, and grinding—was gradually warped across the sandy bar and out into deeper water.

Running aground, an embarrassing event for any captain, was even worse for Inglis in this instance because *Sultana* was traveling that morning in the company of one of the largest warships in His Majesty's North American squadron, HMS *Boston*. *Sultana* had been ordered to accompany *Boston* up the Chesapeake and into the mouth of the Potomac River in order to patrol for smugglers reported to be frequenting Alexandria and Port Tobacco. After *Sultana* was refloated the two vessels made their way uneventfully to Point Lookout at the entrance to the Potomac by the evening of the next day. On the twenty-third, *Sultana* took a pilot on board to help guide the schooner up the river.[4]

During the next two weeks *Sultana* and *Boston* kept busy searching merchant ships sailing up and down the Potomac. On July 24 *Sultana* fired two shots from her half-pound swivel guns to make several passing vessels haul down pennants they were flying in breach of proper naval etiquette. On the same day she searched a sloop from Barbados which was bound for Alexandria with rum and sugar. On the twenty-fifth *Sultana*'s small boat was sent to inspect a sloop from the Susquehanna River, this one laden with market goods for Alexandria. In the first week of August the schooner's men had perhaps their busiest days on the Potomac, stopping and searching a variety of boats—a schooner from Boston carrying rum; a schooner from Port Tobacco loaded with furniture; a schooner from Nantucket headed for Alexandria with dried fish; two vessels from Maryland's "Easterning" (Eastern) Shore, also bound for Alexandria; a brig from Norfolk with tar, pork, and rum in her hold; and sloops from Quantico, George Town, and Antigua carrying rum and sugar to Alexandria! With the boats of *Boston* working just as hard as *Sultana*'s it is doubtful many vessels on the lower Potomac escaped the scrutiny of the Royal Navy in the late summer of 1770.[5]

Despite *Sultana*'s nearly constant activity her captain and crew did find windows of time for recreation and even a rare social call. One such occasion occurred on July 29 when calm winds brought traffic on the Potomac to a halt, providing Lieutenant Inglis and Master David Bruce an opportunity to venture ashore and dine with one of the colonies' most respected figures, Colonel George Washington. Though Inglis and Washington had never met, Inglis's brother Samuel, a prominent Norfolk merchant, had made Washington's acquaintance through their mutual friend Robert Morris.[6]

Outfitted in their finest dress uniforms Bruce and Inglis were rowed to the wharf at Mt. Vernon by several of *Sultana*'s seamen. There they were greeted by Washington's servants, who led them through the plantation's fields, past the newly

This map of the Chesapeake Bay was made by James Mynde for the famous cartographers Charles Mason and Jeremiah Dixon in 1768, just one year before Sultana sailed these same waters. Interestingly the map shows only three port towns on the Chesapeake: Annapolis, Baltimore, and Chester (Chestertown). Courtesy the Maryland State Archives Special Collections (Huntingfield Map Collection), A Map of That Part of America . . . by James Mynde, 1768 (MSA SC 1399-1-74).

*Colonel George Washington must have been a striking figure to Lieutenant John Inglis and Master David Bruce, who dined with the future general and president in July of 1770. This portrait, done less than two years later, shows Washington in his colonel's uniform from the French and Indian War. Courtesy Washington-Custis-Lee Collection, Washington and Lee University, Lexington, Virginia.*

built flour mill, and up to the main house, where Washington awaited their arrival. Even at a distance Bruce and Inglis could see that Colonel Washington was an imposing figure. Standing nearly six feet, four inches tall, Washington towered over all around him. As they drew closer the pair made note of Washington's superbly tailored clothes, his patrician features, and his authoritative manner. This was clearly not a man to be trifled with.

Dinner was a pleasant affair. The food, prepared and served by the slaves of the household, was the finest that Inglis and Bruce had enjoyed in quite some time. The surroundings at Mt. Vernon were among the most comfortable and luxurious to be found in all of North America. Washington was a gracious host and though the focus of conversation occasionally turned to the current troubles between England and the colonies, the colonel, ever the gentleman, made a point of not dwelling upon this potentially unpleasant subject for too long. Dinner was concluded in a few short hours, and after bidding Washington and Mt. Vernon farewell, Inglis and Bruce were escorted down to the wharf where *Sultana*'s boat waited to return them to the schooner.

Though Washington had played it close to the vest with his opinions on colonial matters, Inglis suspected that it was not for lack of interest. Quite to the contrary, everything that Inglis had heard about this man told him that Washington was an ardent supporter of the "American" cause. Neither Washington nor any of the other colonial leaders had yet made the call for outright independence, but Inglis guessed that if and when that day came, this tall Virginian would be involved. If so he and the rest of His Majesty's forces in North America might well have their hands full. A small group of leaders like Washington could make things extremely difficult for the Crown if they put their minds to it.

*Chapter*
*9*

# 2000: The Crew Completes the Hull

The activity and progress at the shipyard didn't take place in a vacuum. To be a functioning organization we had to deal with the facts of business life just like any company. Payroll had to be met, books kept, bills paid, and new sources of funding continuously identified and pursued.

## Building the *Sultana* "Army"

Michael, Joyce, and the board of directors had worked hard over the past two years to build an organization of the size demanded by *Sultana.* Their job was not easy. Like most nonprofits, we weren't exactly flush with cash, and thus could not afford to hire all of the professionals that such a job called for. In the office the administrative staff of *Sultana* was limited to Michael and two extremely capable part-time assistants, Faith Prince and Kathy McAllister. Together this trio took responsibility for directing *Sultana*'s fundraising activities, accounting, public relations, event planning, board and committee structure, and all the myriad chores of an active nonprofit corporation.

To help carry this load, a number of volunteer committees were created to assist with planning and executing various organizational functions. Separate work groups were established for fundraising, public events and relations, budget and finance, and strategic planning. Two years into the project over

sixty individuals were actively participating in one or more of these groups. The high caliber of these people, the vast experience they contributed, and the contacts they made were invaluable. Helping *Sultana* were the likes of retired Washington College president Charles Trout, hotel and gallery owner Carla Massoni, former *Pride of Baltimore* Executive Director and Queen Anne's County Administrator Mark Belton, local bank presidents Ray Tarrach and Mike Macielag, retired White House military adviser Lou Michael, professional media consultants Mickey and Margie Elsberg, Washington College Vice President Joseph Holt, and the printing/graphic design team of Les and Eileen Cioffi, just to name a few! Thanks to these people and dozens of others like them *Sultana* had, in effect, a first-rate consulting firm on permanent retainer.

The committee structure was one of the scores of ways we used to get the local community involved. In early 1998 we established an annual membership program dubbed "Shipmates," and it quickly grew to over fifteen hundred active members. Yellow bumper stickers displaying "*Sultana* Shipmates" became a common sight on the Eastern Shore and were reported to be seen on cars as far away as Texas, Florida, and California.

The shipyard itself rapidly evolved into a community focal point and a source of local pride, with civic groups and clubs using the yard for picnics, meetings, lectures, and fundraisers. Local theater and musical groups even started to schedule

65

*To the casual observer the shipyard often appeared as if it were in total chaos, with tools, wood, and equipment strewn about in a haphazard fashion. To the shipyard crew, however, this apparent mess had, at least most of the time, an underlying organization. For instance bar clamps, chains, and buckets were, as a rule, stored underneath the boat-shed ramp.*

concerts and performances on the small stage used by the ship-wrights for building frames. On Saturdays, and quite often during the week, the shipyard was transformed into a madhouse of visitors, volunteers, and observers. The building process took on the air of an ongoing street party with friends and acquaintances dropping in to see how things were going and often hanging out for a while to watch the action. The number of visitors and the distances they traveled only increased after articles about *Sultana* started to appear in newspapers and magazines. Professional tour organizers from as far away as Philadelphia and Washington began to offer daylong bus trips to visit the shipyard.

Just as they did with the schoolchildren, John and the shipyard crew worked hard to give each visitor a thorough look at *Sultana.* The workers took turns corralling guests into organized groups, fitting them with hard hats, and leading them on a deluxe tour of every nook and cranny of the schooner. Volunteers like Lorraine Whitehair, Jim Wagner, and John's wife Melinda Bookwalter would often dedicate all day Saturday to nothing but tours.

I don't think it is an exaggeration to say that all of us working at the yard loved what we were doing. At no time was this more apparent than when we gave tours. It was almost impossible to get any of us to shut up—not that anyone ever complained. To the contrary, the excitement that was obvious on the faces and in the voices of the shipyard crew proved contagious to the visitors. These ninety-minute tours ended on more than a few occasions with visitors and guides exchanging addresses or going out together for lunch or a beer!

The community spirit and excitement that built up around *Sultana* manifested itself directly in our ability to keep the project going. At this point, with almost no way to earn revenue ourselves, *Sultana* was entirely dependent upon the community for financial support, and the community did not let us down. When Michael and the special events committee organized fundraisers, the *Sultana* family showed up in force. When the shipyard needed help with tools, materials, or expertise, a local businessman or contractor invariably came to the rescue. When we applied to the state for a construction grant, friends of *Sultana* flooded the legislature with letters of support. "I've got more letters about this damn boat sitting on my desk than about all the other bills combined!" one state legislator admiringly complained. "You guys must have an army over there!" And in a sense, we did.

## Ceiling Planking

As spring 2000 began to bloom on the Eastern Shore we had just twelve months to go till launching. Indeed the momentous date had already been picked—Saturday, March 24, 2001. Now that the framing was complete, our next big job was to plank and deck the schooner. Planking is a labor-intensive job that requires a fair number of skilled hands if it is to be accomplished efficiently. In light of this John added another professional shipwright to the building crew, James Knowles, a veteran of both the USS *Constellation* restoration and the building of *Kalmar Nyckel.* Jim was also an experienced carver who would be able to craft *Sultana*'s figurehead and the decorative quarterbadges that would adorn the windows of the captain's cabin.

Around this time we also had our first departure by a shipyard crewmember. Shipwright Richard Emory sadly broke the news that love was leading him to California. We couldn't begrudge him the move. If there is anything that can distract a man from messing about with wooden boats it must be love (though perhaps this depends on the individual). We bid Richard farewell knowing he would be missed, especially for the key role he had played in working with the school groups that visited the shipyard.

Richard's place was filled in an odd but typically *Sultana* fashion. Word quickly spread through the yard of Richard's imminent departure and of the search for a new shipwright. One of the project's most dedicated volunteers, A.J. Kolodziejski, a professional cabinet carpenter and wooden boat enthusiast from Lancaster, Pennsylvania, approached John and Josh to ask if he could fill the spot. We had first met A.J. at the 1998 Wooden Boat Show in St. Michaels, Maryland. Soon afterward, he and his friend Todd Huttenton had started volunteering at the yard, and the two became fast friends and valued work partners of both Josh and John. When A.J. asked if he could come on as a full-time shipwright, in the process agreeing to take a

*Jury-rigged contraptions like the steam box perplexed and fascinated visitors to the shipyard.*

*Volunteer Bill Leverage was a regular member of the shipyard crew, spending almost every Friday and Saturday for two years working at the yard. Here Bill puts the finishing touches on the 22-foot-long steam box in preparation for planking the hull.*

substantial pay cut as well as to separate himself from his family during the week, John and Josh were thrilled. With John, Josh, A.J., and Jim, as well as Stig, Donald, and the rest of the volunteers, we had in place a strong team to take on the task of planking.

White oak had been selected as the material for *Sultana*'s planking. Oak is a strong, durable wood that readily lends itself to steam bending into the tightest of curves. This was important because *Sultana* was a plump little schooner whose lines required that the planks make sweeping bends and tight twists in order to conform to her shapely frames. The raw oak came into the yard as rough-cut "flitches," 18 to 33 feet long, 2½ to 3 inches thick, and 18 to 24 inches wide. The wood was supplied by Schauber's Lumber and Sawmill and had all been cut from local Eastern Shore trees.

The first planks, known as ceiling planks, were fitted on the inside of *Sultana*. In traditional double-sawn construction, planks are affixed on both the inside and outside of the framing. The interior ceiling planks, unlike the exterior planking, are not meant to be watertight. The primary purpose of the ceiling planking is to add additional longitudinal strength to the hull. Historically the ceiling planks were also important because they kept the valuable cargo or provisions away from the wet bilges of the vessel.

Where the plans called for sharp bends, usually at the bow and stern, the planks were first treated to a steam bath for many hours in the shipyard's steam box. The process of steaming makes the fibers of the wood more flexible, thus enabling a plank to take a sharp bend without breaking. This is true, however, only while the plank is still hot. At the shipyard a race against the clock began each time a hot plank was pulled from the steam box. On average the crew had between five and ten minutes to get each 200-pound plank clamped, bent, and perfectly fitted to the hull before the heat and the flexibility gained by steaming was lost.

Facing page: *To provide extra strength to the hull, eighteenth-century vessels like* Sultana *were usually planked on both the outside and inside of the frames.* Sultana's *interior, or ceiling, planks were made from white oak boards that were 2 to 3 inches thick. Each plank was individually steamed and then bent to conform to the inside of the hull.*

*While* Sultana *was being planked, the shipyard's steam box was kept fired on a daily basis for almost three months. Volunteers arrived at the shipyard well before dawn to start the fire so that the steam box was up to temperature by the time the rest of the crew arrived.*

*Shipwrights A.J. Kolodziejski, Richard Emory, and Josh Herman load the first section of* Sultana's *white oak planking into the steam box. Steaming the hull planks made the wood flexible enough to be wrapped around the sharp bends of* Sultana's *bow without breaking.*

As the ceiling planks cooled, the fibers in the wood once again became rigid, thus fixing the plank into its new curved shape. The morning after being steamed and fitted each plank was removed from the hull, primed on the backside with a special preservative, slathered with a thick bedding tar, and permanently fastened to the frames.

Fastening the planks to the hull was a process that in many ways was more labor-intensive than the planking itself. In our planning sessions with the architect and the Coast Guard it had been agreed that a combination of traditional "trunnels" (treenails or wooden nails) and modern silica-bronze lag bolts would be used to secure *Sultana*'s planks. John had opted for employing a high proportion of trunnels both for historic purposes and because in many applications traditional wooden nails still have advantages over modern metal fastenings. Wooden fastenings are lighter than metal and do not corrode or conduct electricity. In the long run employing trunnels would help to lengthen the life of the planks because the trunnel, being wood, would flex and move with the wooden plank. Metal fasteners, in contrast, have the potential to create "hard spots" around which the relatively softer and constantly flexing wooden planks will wear.

In colonial times trunnels were easy to find. Today they are not. Months before planking was to begin, several crewmembers, led by volunteers Jim Wagner and Bill Bayne, dedicated themselves full time to fabricating the trunnels—approximately 10,000 of them—that would be needed just for the planking. It was an overwhelming job. Starting with raw Osage logs, it took Jim and Bill a full eight-hour day to make 200 trunnel "blanks"—2-foot lengths of Osage that were 1¼-inch square. It was critical that the trunnels be almost completely devoid of moisture so they wouldn't shrink once they were driven into the schooner. To make certain of this, the trunnel blanks were stacked in a heated drying room and "baked" for two to three months until their moisture content was below 6 percent. Once dry, the blanks were sawn to 1⅛-inch square and then run through a dowel cutter to produce a round wooden

*Facing page: In order to make certain that no metal fastenings were struck when drilling the shaft hole, the entire aft end of the schooner was initially fastened exclusively with wooden nails. Only after the shaft hole was bored did A.J. Kolodziejski go back to tie the framing together with bronze rods and bolts.*

*Sultana's interior, or ceiling, planking sweeps up and in toward almost a single point in the bow of the vessel.*

*Crucial to the integrity of* Sultana's *hull was the ability to mill the wooden trunnels (the hull fasteners) to a precise diameter. If a trunnel was too small in diameter it might work loose under stress. If a trunnel was too thick it might split the surrounding wood into which it was driven. A caliper was used periodically to ensure that the diameter of the trunnels was within an allowed tolerance.*

72   Schooner *Sultana*

nail exactly 1 inch in diameter. All things considered it took about ten minutes to fabricate each trunnel or over sixteen hundred man-hours to make all 10,000!

The ceiling planking went along quickly and was mostly complete by May. Rather than moving directly to the exterior planking, John and the crew decided instead to shift work to the decks, rails, and transom. There was concern that the heat of the summer might cause the exterior planks to shrink after they had been fastened. This would make the planks harder to caulk and could potentially cause the schooner to leak badly when she was launched. The rest of the planking would have to wait until fall, just a few months before the scheduled launch.

## Summer 2000

For the summer of 2000 the shipyard crew broke up into several teams. A.J. and summer apprentice Ken Castelli turned their attention to the decking; volunteers Herb Wilkinson, Tom Fulton, Ted Hornaday, and Mickey Elsberg followed right behind them with cotton caulk; Josh and volunteer Bill Leverage worked to finish out the transom; Jim Knowles took care of the rails, catheads (part of the anchoring gear), and the schooner's carvings; and Stig and Donald started to build the floors and bulkheads in *Sultana*'s interior. It was a busy shipyard.

With March 24, 2001, looming ever closer John and I focused more of our attention on *Sultana*'s rig, finishing details, and operating systems. We both knew that the ultimate quality of *Sultana* as a historic reproduction, not to mention her utility as a functioning sailing vessel, would depend greatly upon our attention to these items. A modern engine, exhaust system, electrical system, galley, and head all had to be incorporated into *Sultana*'s original design while care was taken that they did not destroy it. Historic features and systems of the original vessel, including interior carpentry, the ship's wood-burning brick stove, and the rig all had to be researched, recreated, and made safe and functional.

*Facing page: The inside of* Sultana's *unfinished hull took on an almost mystical quality as the planking neared completion. Stepping down the ladder into the hold was almost like entering another world.*

*Students of all ages and backgrounds found their way to the shipyard. Here Josh Herman conveys the finer points of planking to shipbuilding school student Margie Elsberg. Well over a hundred students like Margie participated in weeklong shipbuilding classes at the yard.*

*In order to provide an added measure of safety and to comply with U.S. Coast Guard regulations, a watertight collision bulkhead was added toward the bow of* Sultana. *Should the schooner ever suffer a collision and develop a significant leak in the bow, the bulkhead will help to retain the watertight integrity of the aft two-thirds of the vessel.*

The Sultana *shipyard was no ordinary boatyard. While* Sultana *was under construction the yard hosted numerous social and cultural events including concerts, plays, and even a wedding. Here the Francis Elliot Country Band plays at a volunteer appreciation party.*

*Whether during a party such as the one shown above or on any average work day, the shipyard was generally awash with visitors eager to get a glance of* Sultana *under construction.*

*Visitors to the shipyard found the color of the Osage orange wood so unusual that they often wanted to take a piece of it home with them. With the assistance of volunteers, visitors were allowed to rummage through the scrap pile to find a suitable memento.*

The rig was by far the biggest of these jobs. Thanks to the schooner's logbooks and a healthy body of previous academic work, a fair amount was known about *Sultana*'s rig. Especially helpful to us was an article by Dana McCalip in the *Nautical Research Journal* that described the rig of a typical colonial schooner, using *Sultana* as an example. With this historic and academic information in hand, the task of developing *Sultana*'s rig was given to architect Tom Fake at the Benford Design Group. Tom performed an engineering study on the historic rig and created a basic plan and a set of engineering parameters. The next step was to flesh out the details of the hardware, rigging leads, and materials. To help with this effort, two new people were added to the *Sultana* team: rigger Mark Roesner, who would be responsible for directing the creation of the rig, and *Pride of Baltimore II* captain Jan Miles, who provided input and advice based upon his extensive experience sailing traditional vessels.

Constant thought was given to the trade-off between historical accuracy and modern safety and utility. Building *Sultana*'s rig exactly as it had been in 1768 would have been impractical and perhaps even dangerous. It must be remembered that the original *Sultana* had a crew of twenty-five and according to the logbooks these men spent a great amount of time maintaining the rig. Since we were intent on spending most of our time with *Sultana* teaching children, we needed rigging solutions that would reduce the demands of regular rig maintenance. The most significant difference between the historic *Sultana*'s rig and the new *Sultana*'s rig would be the inclusion of modern synthetic rigging materials that retained a traditional appearance while adding strength and durability.

Work began on the rig in the summer of 2000 with the fabrication of the shrouds and stays, or standing rigging—those lines that would support the masts. Historically the core of the shrouds would have been composed of hemp rope that was selectively "wormed, parceled, and served." This three-step process was done to protect the rope from chafe and weather. In "worming," a thin line is placed between the strands of a rope to fill out the shape and form a smooth outer surface. "Parceling" adds protection as strips of canvas or other material (sometimes coated with tar for more weatherproofing) are wound around the

*Sultana's smaller spars—her booms, gaffs, yards, and so on—were made using a technique known as "bird's mouth" lamination. First, eight long tapered rectangular pieces of wood were sawn. Next, a 45-degree notch (the bird's mouth) was sawn in the narrow face of each piece. The eight pieces of wood were then arranged in a circle and glued together. Here a cutoff from the end of a yard shows how the eight pieces interconnect.*

*The original* Sultana *boasted eight half-pound swivel guns. Resembling a small cannon mounted on a rotating swivel, the swivel gun was used historically for signaling and as a deadly antipersonnel weapon. When the first replica swivel gun arrived at the shipyard, volunteer Jim Wagner, an avid black-powder enthusiast, went straight to work building a temporary Osage carriage so that the weapon could be fired.*

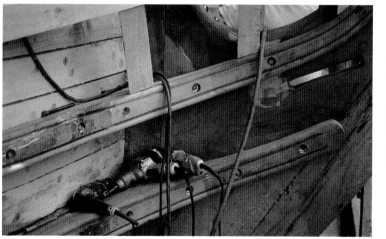

*Sultana's most elaborate and artistic carpentry is found at the bow of the schooner. A series of decorative and functional brackets, or cheek knees, provide* Sultana *with a distinctive look usually reserved for larger, more important vessels.*

*Experienced sailor and rigger Mark Roesner served as chief rigger for* Sultana. *Here Mark "serves"* Sultana's *forestay.*

*Historically,* Sultana *was, for the most part, very simple and unadorned. One of the few purely decorative details on the original schooner was a series of beaded planks that ran around the top of the hull. In the bow of the new schooner curved lengths of bright yellow Osage were used to fabricate this detail.*

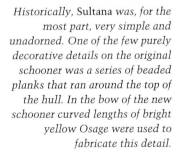

rope, in preparation for serving. Finally, the rope is "served": small cord is wrapped around the rope tightly, keeping the coils very close together. *Sultana*'s new shrouds would be similar except that the core would be galvanized wire rope rather than hemp, and the parceling and serving would be applied to the entire length of each shroud in order to conceal and protect the wire rope. Under the guidance of Mark Roesner, volunteers Jim Wagner, David Roberts, and Ted Hornaday spent the best part of two months parceling the shrouds with tarred canvas and then serving them with thousands of feet of jute line.

Shortly after the launch, when the finished shrouds would be installed on the schooner, they would be looped around the heads of the masts and led down to both sides of the hull. The tail of each shroud would be secured by a deadeye/lanyard (block and line) arrangement to an iron chain plate bolted securely to the side of the schooner. We were extremely lucky to find a talented craftsman, Norris White, who generously agreed to assist with the fabrication of the schooner's wooden deadeyes as well as much of the rest of the wooden rigging gear. A retired carpenter, World War II veteran of the Eighty-second Airborne Division, and a world-class wood turner, Norris had learned about *Sultana* from his sister who lives in Chestertown. On a whim she had given him some scrap Osage from the shipyard which he promptly returned as exquisitely turned bowls, vases, and plates to be sold in the shipyard store. Impressed by his work we sent him a block of Osage with a drawing of a deadeye. Sure enough one week later Norris had produced a perfect reproduction of our drawing. Ultimately, he fabricated no fewer than 150 separate parts for *Sultana*. His only remuneration was a promise that he would sail on the completed schooner.

About a half-hour's drive from Norris's Sellersville, Pennsylvania, workshop another craftsperson was hard at work producing additional components for *Sultana*'s rig. Blacksmith Kelly Smyth was contracted to forge *Sultana*'s custom ironwork including the schooner's chain plates. A former blacksmith at both Colonial Williamsburg and Mystic Seaport Museum and a veteran of two other vessel reproductions, *Susan Constant* and *Kalmar Nyckel*, Kelly brought to *Sultana* over twenty years of experience fashioning eighteenth-century hardware.

*Each of* Sultana's *two lower masts (mainmast and foremast) is supported by a series of eight cables known as shrouds. Originally these shrouds would have been made from laid hemp rope. For safety and ease of maintenance, the new* Sultana *employs galvanized wire rope shrouds, each painstakingly wound in traditional fiber rope to protect it and give it an authentic appearance. Volunteer Jim Wagner spent the best part of two months using a "serving mallet" to encase* Sultana's *shrouds.*

*Wire splicing is an exacting and tedious job that requires both strength and skill. The galvanized wire rope used for* Sultana's *shrouds was composed of sixteen individual strands, each of which had to be precisely unraveled and rewoven in order to make an "eye splice." Rigger Mark Roesner often spent the best part of a day executing a single splice.*

*Although he rarely visited the shipyard, Norris White was one of* Sultana's *most productive and valued volunteers. Working out of his Sellersville, Pennsylvania, workshop, Norris produced hundreds of deadeyes and other wooden rigging gear used to connect* Sultana's *shrouds to the hull.*

*The serving mallets used in the rigging of* Sultana *differ little from their eighteenth-century counterparts. The most significant addition to the modern serving mallet is a rotating spool used to hold hundreds of feet of traditional marline. In the eighteenth century a small boy holding a ball of marline would have substituted for the spool.*

*Upon their arrival at the shipyard, the deadeyes made by Norris White were placed into a solution of linseed oil, turpentine, and pine tar and left to soak for several months. The soaking process helps to prevent the deadeyes from drying out and cracking even after long years of exposure to the sun.*

Kelly was a purist and worked out of a true eighteenth-century blacksmith shop in Concordville, Pennsylvania. There was not a single modern tool to be found in Kelly's shop—not even an electric light or outlet. The coal fire in the stone forge was maintained with the help of a pair of 9-foot-long leather bellows that had to be inflated by hand several times each minute. Coal dust hung in the air and covered virtually every square inch of the shop. As clean as Kelly might be when she arrived in the morning, by the end of the day it would have been hard to distinguish her from a West Virginia miner.

The ironwork required for *Sultana* was relatively heavy for Kelly's small forge. To heat and shape the 1- to 2-inch thick iron required hour upon hour of pulling the bellows and then striking countless blows with a heavy sledge. To speed the process and save Kelly from utter exhaustion, volunteers from the shipyard traveled back and forth to Concordville where they served as assistants. Though the help of the volunteers sped up the work, we realized that the operation would be even more efficient if we could find a couple of volunteers to take over as full-time apprentices. Mickey Elsberg and George Griffin eagerly agreed to fill the part and soon they and Kelly were an inseparable and very productive team. The trio's work was aided with the "cheating" help of George Kreshock, owner of a local precision machine shop, who saved Kelly, Mickey, and George weeks of hammering by premachining the iron pieces in his high-tech shop.

In addition to Mark, Norris, and Kelly, there were several other craftspeople hard at work fabricating portions of *Sultana*'s rig in the summer of 2000. In Nova Scotia, Arthur Dauphine and his team were building two hundred ash and bronze blocks for *Sultana*'s running rigging. In Rock Hall, Maryland, welder Martin Legg and ironworker Alfred Jacquette were fashioning iron straps for the deadeyes. In Boothbay Harbor, Maine, sailmaker Nat Wilson was laying out the panels for *Sultana*'s sails. If everything went according to plan the work of all these craftspeople would come together in the weeks after *Sultana*'s launch. All the parts would be assembled like a giant model kit. Only then would we know if everything had been planned and executed just right.

*Iron was an expensive commodity in 1768 and* Sultana, *like most other eighteenth-century merchant vessels, employed it only where absolutely necessary. In order to make the schooner true to its time period all of the visible ironwork on the new* Sultana *was hand made or hand finished at a traditional forge. Working in her forge in Concordville, Pennsylvania, blacksmith Kelly Smyth fabricated hundreds of items for the schooner.*

## Thinking about the Future

As construction barreled forward in the summer of 2000 everyone's field of vision, including my own, began to narrow considerably. The pressure to finish the vessel properly, on schedule, and within budget grew greater each day, and the time available to work on nonconstruction-related planning diminished proportionately. From a business standpoint we were now coming into the most perilous period of the project. In less than twelve months we would have an operational vessel and a payroll full of sailing crew, educators, and administrative staff, yet we still had no clients—not a single group of students with a commitment to sail on *Sultana*. If action wasn't taken quickly to change this state of affairs we would end up having built a big, beautiful schooner that would do nothing but sit at the dock.

As a result of our work at the beginning of the project, we remained confident that from a business perspective we were right on target with our future plans. *Sultana* had all the characteristics of a first-class schoolship, and there was a demonstrated demand for the type of education we proposed to offer. Next we needed to make the transformation from concept to product. Put simply we had to figure out exactly how this "schoolship" concept would work.

Since all the members of our team already had their hands full with fundraising and/or building we decided to make an addition to our crew by adding a director of education, someone whose sole responsibility would be to refine *Sultana*'s curriculum and market her onboard programs to school groups. Filling this new slot was Chris Cerino, another veteran of Echo Hill Outdoor School as well as an experienced classroom teacher. Having worked side by side with Chris for three years at Echo Hill, I couldn't have been happier. He was passionate about history, loved the water, and was as dynamic and creative a teacher as I had ever seen. I had little doubt that he would make the perfect education leader for *Sultana*.

*Facing page: The daunting job of making* Sultana's *traditional sails was contracted to sailmaker Nat Wilson of Booth Bay Harbor, Maine. The work was done using a combination of modern and historic tools, materials, and techniques.*

*While parts of* Sultana's *sails were machine sewn, the more visible sections, such as the traditional three-strand boltrope ringing the edge of each sail, was hand sewn, in this case by the master sailmaker himself, Nat Wilson.*

*Hundreds of hours went into fashioning the hand-sewn details of* Sultana's *sails. This sailmaker's bench in Nat Wilson's sail loft displays some of the common and the unique tools employed by the traditional sailmaker.*

Thin sheets of lauan (¼-inch plywood) were regularly used to fabricate templates for large timbers. Repeatedly fitting and shaping the light and workable plywood was far easier than the alternative of fitting and shaping a heavy oak or Osage timber. Once the pattern was made to fit perfectly it was a simple process to transfer the shape from the pattern to the working timber.

Sultana's hull is graced by three carvings: a figurehead at the bow directly under the bowsprit, and two quarter badges, decorative carvings around the windows located in the hull near the stern. The design for the quarter badges, shown here being carved by Jim Knowles, was taken directly from the Royal Navy's original 1768 survey of Sultana.

In certain instances members of the shipyard crew became self-educated eighteenth-century artisans. An example of hands-on improvisation based upon historic records was the process used to fabricate Sultana's lead-lined deck scuppers. A small team of volunteers spent several days recreating the craft of leadsmithing through trial and error. Eventually they became adept at hammering, bending, and fastening protective lead to various parts of the vessel.

*The most impressive piece of machinery on* Sultana *is her massive oak and Osage windlass shown here at different stages of construction. Employed when hauling in the anchor, the octagonal, horizontal windlass is supported by two vertical posts of Osage, as seen in the photographs.*

Sultana's weather deck is composed of four separate levels. From bow to stern these sections are called the foredeck, the middle deck or waist, the quarterdeck, and the poop deck. Historically each deck had a specific purpose. The unplanked foredeck and partially planked middle deck shown here were used to haul anchor tackle and carry cargo respectively. The quarterdeck and poop deck (not shown) were generally reserved for the captain and other officers so they could watch over and direct the activities of the crew.

According to Sultana's logbooks the vessel usually sailed with a significant amount of stone ballast in the bilge to improve the stability of the vessel. Lead weights, like those shown here, serve much the same purpose in the new schooner. The majority of the new Sultana's ballast was salvaged out of the bilge of the decommissioned U.S. Navy hospital ship Comfort.

Chris came on board in July and by Thanksgiving he had already made huge progress. Our previously rudimentary curriculum outlines had been transformed into detailed educational battle plans, each tailored to complement prescribed state public school educational goals. Chris also began to develop full-blown *Sultana*-inspired classroom units in colonial history and environmental science. With the addition of these classroom units students would now spend an entire month working with *Sultana*, not just a single day sailing on the schooner.

Gradually the work Chris put into developing *Sultana*'s onboard programs began to pay off. Teachers who had previously been impressed with the physical vessel now began to appreciate how a trip with their students on *Sultana* could complement and reinforce what they were doing in the classroom. As time passed the names of schools making arrangements to sail on *Sultana* began to fill up the previously blank spaces on our 2001 sailing calendar. While we still had a long way to go before *Sultana* was a smoothly running schoolship, we had taken the first, important steps in that long, perhaps never-ending, process.

## Exterior Planking— Josh and A.J. Rise to the Occasion

The weeks of October are usually among the year's most beautiful on Maryland's Eastern Shore. The season is marked by annual rituals that recur with comforting predictability. On October 1 the watermen exchange their crabbing gear for hand tongs and make their way out to the oyster bars for the first day of a new season. The vanguard of the wintering Canada goose population arrives just as the summering ospreys strike camp and begin their long migration south. By the end of the month the leaves have turned to brilliant fall shades and the farmers have taken in the year's crop, leaving the fields open and barren for the coming winter.

For most of the summer of 2000 the *Sultana* crew had been spread around the shipyard, working separately on different areas of the schooner. As the calendar rolled over to October the shipwrights and volunteers knew it was time to finish up their

*Because scores of different people worked on the schooner at different times it was imperative to find ways to communicate information to all the members of the work crew. The shipwrights and volunteers often wrote notes directly on the vessel in order to impart an important fact to the next shift.*

*On rare occasions the shipwrights were forced to use epoxy to laminate pieces of wood together in order to achieve the large working timber sizes they required. This was done begrudgingly and only after an exhaustive search had been made for a suitable nonlaminated timber. Here A.J. Kolodziejski laminates three pieces of Osage orange for use as* Sultana's *foredeck rail cap.*

86 Schooner *Sultana*

summer projects so that we could come together for our last significant communal project. It was time to plank the bottom.

It would be hard to overestimate the importance of the bottom planking. The almost 3-inch-thick layer of wood planks covering the submerged portion of *Sultana*'s hull would keep the schooner safely afloat. Done correctly, the planking would provide years of dry sailing. A sloppy job would result in a leaky, wet, and potentially dangerous vessel with chronic maintenance problems.

As with the interior ceiling planking, white oak was the material of choice for the bottom planking. Thinking ahead, John had obtained 7,000 board feet of oak especially for the bottom planks back in the fall of 1998. The carefully stacked winter-cut oak had been drying in the back corner of the shipyard for almost two years. This was an important detail as oak, like all woods, shrinks as it dries. If the planking material was not sufficiently low in moisture content, the fastened planks could shrink apart from each other leaving large open gaps—not a good thing in the bottom of a boat!

The first step in the planking process was to "line off" the hull to determine the number of strakes, or rows, of planking that would be required. The task of lining off fell to Josh who in short order calculated that *Sultana*'s bottom would require twenty strakes of planking (6 to 8 inches wide) on each side, port and starboard. Since each strake would have to be composed of 3 to 4 planks (in order to run the length of the schooner) this meant that *Sultana*'s bottom would be composed of approximately 150 individual oak planks, some weighing as much as several hundred pounds.

With the hull lined off John divided the shipyard crew into three teams: port and starboard planking crews of four volunteers, led respectively by Josh and A.J., and a team of fasteners to follow behind the planking crews. Through November and

*Whenever two pieces of wood were fastened together, each piece was first painted with protective antifouling paint and then coated with tar.*

*When it came time to hang a steamed plank, the process required the strength and attention of every worker in the yard. Planks were often steamed for about two hours to render them flexible enough to be bent around the hull frames. Once a plank was removed from the steam box, the shipyard crew had to work quickly and efficiently to get the plank into place before it cooled and lost its ability to bend. Generally the working time was no more than five minutes.*

Facing page: *The first plank affixed to the outside of* Sultana's *hull was the "wale plank" or "wale strake." Situated just above the vessel's designed waterline, the wale strake at four inches of thickness is almost twice as thick as the rest of the hull planking. Once the wale strake is in place the remainder of the hull is "lined off" to indicate how the planks will be arranged on the frames. Here A.J. Kolodziejski and John Swain line off the topmost plank or sheer strake of the hull.*

*Different types of fastenings were used to secure the white oak hull planks to the Osage orange frames. At the ends, or butts, of each plank, half-inch-diameter silica-bronze lag bolts were used to provide extra strength and holding power. In between the butts, wooden trunnels were the primary fasteners. Looking at the partially completed side of the hull it is easy to identify the bronze bolts by their countersunk heads.*

*The purpose of the planking rabbet becomes much more clear once the frames have been added to the keel. It is easy to see here how the edge of the bottom-most plank, known as the garboard plank, will lock into the keel.*

December the daily work routine of these three teams varied little. The crews followed a repetitive five-step process: spiling, cutting, beveling, steaming, and clamping.

Spiling was perhaps the most crucial and complicated step in the process. In preparation for cutting each plank, the lines Josh had drawn on the three-dimensional hull of *Sultana* had to be precisely transferred onto the two-dimensional flat surface of a rough-cut slab of oak. To accomplish this task the shipwrights used a thin 25-foot-long wooden batten, which they temporarily fastened to the hull along the lines of a plank. With the assistance of an overgrown scribing compass (like those used in geometry class with the size multiplied by a factor of twenty) Josh and A.J. transferred the plank lines from the schooner onto the face of the batten. Once the lines had been transferred the batten was removed from the hull and placed onto an oak plank where the process could be repeated in reverse so that an exact copy of the planking lines on the hull would be made onto the face of the oak plank.

When each plank had been scribed, it could then be sawn to shape, beveled on one edge to accommodate caulking, steamed, bent, and clamped into place on the hull. On a good day each planking crew could cut and hang two or three planks.

Generally no fewer than twelve people at a time worked on planking and fastening *Sultana*. Of these at least nine were volunteers with little or no boatbuilding experience. Overseeing this process was an extremely important job. In an ideal situation it would have demanded everyone's undivided attention. Unfortunately building a schooner on a nonprofit budget rarely, if ever, produces ideal work situations.

The obvious person to take charge of the bottom planking was, of course, John. With over thirty years of work on traditional wooden vessels, John had more experience than the rest of the shipyard crew combined. Ironically, however, as we neared the end of hull construction John's wealth of experience required that he spend less and less time actually working on the vessel. Increasingly both John and I found ourselves pulled away from daily operations by the demands of planning and design associated with rigging, engine, tanks, hardware, and so on—including oversight of the legion of subcontractors involved.

*The edges of each plank were planed at an angle. Once the planks were in position, the planed edges created caulking seams into which cotton caulk and tarred oakum could be driven. In this photo shipwright A.J. Kolodziejski takes great care to plane a clean and consistent bevel.*

*Drilling holes in* Sultana's *hull was almost always a two-person job. One person operated the drill while a "spotter" stood back to make sure the drill bit was boring into the hull at the proper angle. Due to the enormous number of fastenings in the hull, great care was taken when drilling to make certain that the drill bit did not encounter a previously placed rod or bolt.*

*Osage orange and white oak, the two principal woods used for* Sultana, *are easy to differentiate, even for the untrained eye. The most noticeable difference between the woods is color—the two are shown contrasting here in* Sultana's *billethead. Osage is bright orange while oak is light tan. Osage is also significantly heavier and harder than oak. Here shipwright Jim Knowles uses an electric hand planer to put the finishing touches on* Sultana's *billethead.*

*Shipwright and carver James Knowles invested over a month and a half of his time in the construction of* Sultana's *decorative bow. Here he reviews his progress with John Swain.*

Luckily Josh and A.J. were there to step in. Both were excellent shipwrights, and even though planking *Sultana* was a much more difficult job than either man had ever been involved with, they both threw themselves into the project and soon had the task well in hand. Under their guidance rows of precisely fitted planks were methodically made fast to the hull. Each day without delay, the unplanked portion of *Sultana*'s skeleton grew smaller and smaller.

Like all good managers Josh and A.J. knew the importance of having well-defined goals for the work crew. They also knew the value of a good challenge. Being the pessimist of the group I had estimated it would take until the middle of January to complete *Sultana*'s planking. Eager to best this estimate the pair set a goal for the crew to finish the planking no later then December 31. For good measure the date was publicly announced and a special celebration planned so that there could be no failure without a fair amount of humiliation.

In the end no one was required to eat crow. The goal of finishing *Sultana*'s planking by the end of the year was met with a day to spare. To commemorate the accomplishment a special "whiskey trunnel," was prepared. The trunnel, signed by every member of the shipyard crew, would be the very last one driven into *Sultana*'s hull. At the appointed hour each of the shipwrights and volunteers stepped up to the hull and, after taking a ceremonial shot of whiskey at Josh's urging, took a whack at the trunnel. Fifty whacks later it was all over. *Sultana* had a bottom.

*Chapter*
*10*

# January 1771: Newport Becomes a Hotbed

From the moment he saw *Sultana*'s small boats making their way across the harbor toward his vessel, Thomas Roberts knew that this wasn't going to be his day. It was Monday, January 21, 1771. Roberts, a twenty-three-year-old Welshman, was signed on board a small merchant sloop that was riding at anchor while making a winter stopover in Newport Harbor, Rhode Island. The sloop's captain and the rest of the crew were clearly annoyed at the prospect of being boarded and rummaged by *Sultana*'s Royal Navy crew; still they knew that they had little to fear. In her hold the small vessel carried nothing more than ballast—not the smuggled goods for which the navy sailors were searching. Once *Sultana*'s crew realized this they would quickly be on their way leaving the sloop and her crew in peace.

For Roberts, however, *Sultana*'s approaching boats were a matter of somewhat more intense concern. Making an effort not to alert his shipmates Roberts quietly slipped belowdecks and worked his way forward to the bosun's storage closet. Hiding there among the sloop's spare canvas he could clearly hear the voices of *Sultana*'s men as they tied the schooner's small boats alongside. David Bruce, *Sultana*'s master, was leading the boarding party that morning. Roberts heard his voice rising above the general confusion as he ordered the sloop's crew to assemble on the port side of the deck. There they were placed under armed guard while the rest of *Sultana*'s men made ready to search the sloop for contraband.

Despite protestations from the sloop's captain that his vessel was sailing with only ballast, Bruce insisted on making a thorough examination of the hold. The Americans were a crafty lot, Bruce well knew, and a seemingly innocent load of shingle ballast could, if arranged correctly, hide a multitude of illegal goods. Working from the stern forward *Sultana*'s men systematically examined every nook and hollow of the sloop's interior. The only way Roberts could avoid detection was if Bruce would believe the words of the sloop's captain and call off the search before *Sultana*'s men worked forward and found the hiding place. Unfortunately for Roberts this was not to be.

On deck Bruce could hear raised voices and scuffling emanating from below. "What's going on down there?" he barked through the main cargo hatch, making sure all the while to keep a close eye on the sloop's crew lest they use this as an opportunity to make trouble.

"Mr. Bruce, we have a long-lost friend of ours down here who I am sure is very eager to see you," replied *Sultana*'s gunner's mate, Thomas Nicholson, in his thick Scottish accent.

In short order Roberts was brought on deck and presented before David Bruce. "*Sultana* hasn't been the same without you Roberts," Bruce said sarcastically. "I am sure Lieutenant Inglis will be as glad to see you as I am. I expect that he might even have a welcome home present in store for you. I only hope that the skin on your back is thick enough to accept it properly."

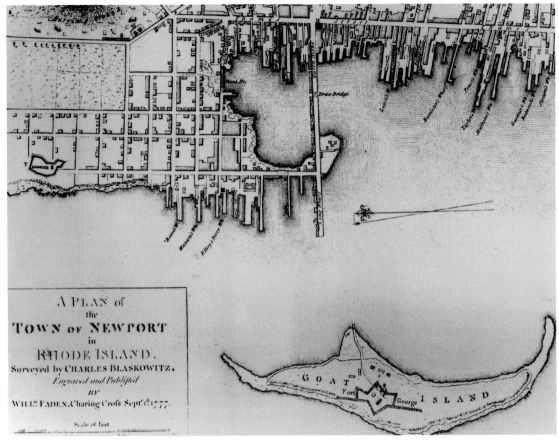

*Prior to the American Revolution the port of Newport, Rhode Island, was known as one of the most rebellious-minded cities in the thirteen colonies. Part of this reputation sprang from incidents like that in which* Sultana *played a role on the evening of January 21, 1771. Outraged by the seizure of a Royal Navy deserter by* Sultana's *crew, angry citizens of Newport surrounded the schooner in small boats and threatened to burn her to her waterline. Courtesy the Newport Historical Society (01.952).*

With that Roberts was manhandled down to one of the awaiting small boats and Bruce's boarding party cast off from the sloop and made its way back to *Sultana.*

Of the many men who had run from *Sultana* in the past two years, Roberts was one of the very few who had been apprehended. Lieutenant Inglis, constantly struggling to retain his crew, would have little choice but to make an example of Roberts by publicly and harshly punishing him for his desertion. It was an aspect of his job that he did not particularly enjoy, but it was nonetheless essential for maintaining order on his vessel, even as the colonies around her seemed to be spiraling headlong into lawlessness and rebellion.

Word of Roberts's bad luck spread quickly into Newport, a hotbed of sailors and smugglers that was already seething with resentment at the heavy hand of the Royal Navy. It was winter, and the town's taverns and boardinghouses were filled with idle seamen biding their time while waiting for the fair winds of spring. The story of a sailor's seizure at the hands of *Sultana's* crew, exaggerated no doubt after the consumption of copious amounts of alcohol, was just the sort of prodding that was required to arouse this hornets' nest.

Within hours Newport was in an uproar. Bands of sailors and other assorted riffraff made their way from tavern to tavern imploring their fellow seamen not to let this injustice pass without response. Within the angry mob vague but impassioned plans were hastily made to rescue Thomas Roberts and to burn *Sultana*, the hated symbol of British oppression.

Nearby several of *Sultana's* crew, who had come ashore to secure supplies, overheard the plans for their schooner's demise being hatched in Newport's back alleys. Quietly but quickly they made they made their way back to the harbor and the schooner's boat. Rowing out to warn the anchored *Sultana* the men watched as the citizens of Newport assembled longboats, torches, and even the occasional musket in preparation for an evening assault.

"Had it really come to this?" thought Inglis as the shore party informed him of the events transpiring in the city. Without question or hesitation Inglis was an avid Tory, loyal to the Crown. Still, North America was the land of his birth, as well as that of his parents and grandparents. He did not relish the idea of fighting and perhaps killing other Americans—even this misguided, drunken rabble of Newport. Hoping that if he publicly demonstrated his schooner's readiness to fight he might be able to avoid doing so, Inglis ordered his men to clear *Sultana's* decks and to load the schooner's swivel guns and small arms.

As night fell Inglis ordered all hands on deck. The men did their best to bundle themselves against the cold January night while they waited to see what if anything would emerge from the wharves of Newport. Nightfall only served to embolden the assembled men of the city—at least to a point. Their anonymity ensured by the darkness, the unruly mob boldly assaulted *Sultana* with verbal threats and taunts. Throughout Inglis and his men remained calm. With their linstocks lit and their muskets loaded, it would take significantly more than harsh words from a drunken crowd to force them to release Thomas Roberts or to surrender the decks of their vessel.

Through the course of the evening and into the early morning hours of the next day, particularly bold groups of Newport rebels rowed out into the harbor to probe and assess *Sultana's* defenses. Each time they were met with a stern and unwavering warning from the deck of the schooner: "Stand off or prepare to be fired upon." Eventually the mob—cold, tired, and inebriated—lost their passion for the cause and one by one drifted back up the alleys of Newport to find a warm, comfortable place to sleep. By morning the town was quiet and the crew of *Sultana* could stand down and take a well-deserved rest.

Upon reflection Inglis realized that *Sultana* had never been in any great danger. Still, the events of that January day in Newport were enough to make him worry about what the future might hold. *Sultana* had faced a drunken and hastily assembled mob. As would be expected her crew of organized, well-armed sailors had proved to be more than a match for the mob. Inglis wondered how the outcome might differ were they ever to face a well-planned assault from a determined group of sober colonists. Though some of his colleagues in the Royal Navy and the British Army were quick to dismiss the military potential of the Americans, Inglis was not so sure. The colonists were a hardy, clever, and self-reliant people. If it came to blows they would be fighting on their home soil with the vastness of an entire continent to draw from and in which to hide. The British on the other hand would be fighting on unfamiliar ground with a supply line almost three thousand miles long. Inglis could only hope that matters with the colonists were resolved before it came to that.

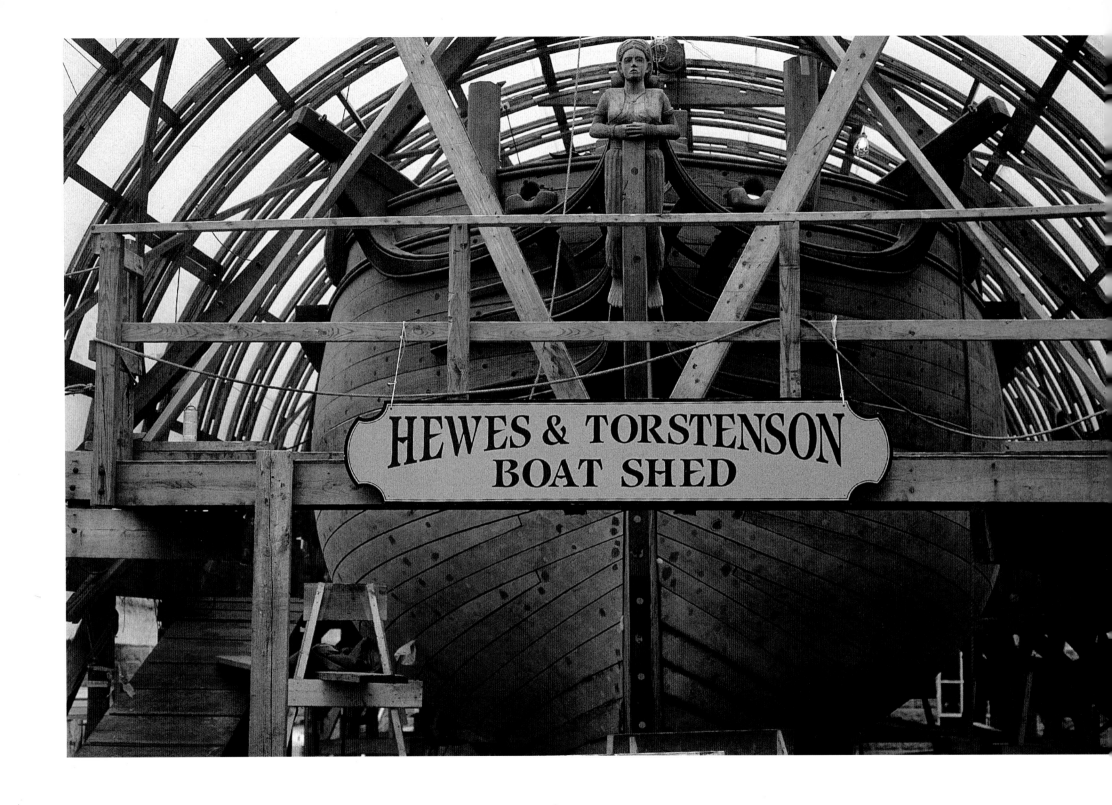

*Chapter*
## *11*

# 2001: The Army Launches *Sultana*

Tuesday, January 2, 2001, 7:00 A.M. A simple sign scribbled with a marker and crudely nailed to the wall greeted the shipyard crew as we dragged our New Year's–weary bodies into the workshop for our first morning meeting of the new millennium. "58 Days!!!" The message was short but said it all. Just fifty-eight workdays stood between us and March 23 when, ready or not, *Sultana* would be rolled out from beneath her shed and hauled down to the river to await her launch.

## The Home Stretch

The date was firm. Building a historic wooden schooner three blocks from the water in a town that has no maritime infrastructure allowed no flexibility in the schedule. Moving *Sultana* to the river and putting her in the water—what three years previously we had thought would be a relatively easy problem to overcome—was turning out to be a major undertaking. Seventy-five trained professionals and over $30 million of equipment (including three tugboats, a 100-ton hydraulic trailer, and the U.S.

Army's largest floating crane) were scheduled to descend on Chestertown the fourth weekend in March to help move and launch *Sultana*. Assembling the required men and equipment had been a Herculean task. If we fell behind on construction and overshot the appointed date it might be a long time before we got a second opportunity to put *Sultana* into the water.

With the schooner's planking complete the main tasks that remained before launch included caulking the bottom planking, fabricating and installing the rudder, shaping the schooner's two lower masts and bowsprit, and putting a few coats of paint onto the sides and bottom of the hull. Of course those were just the big jobs. The list of smaller but equally crucial items was ten times as long.

In terms of total man-hours, caulking *Sultana* was the most substantial task that lay before us. Even with the great work that Josh, A.J., and the rest of the crew had done to fit the bottom planking tightly, it was still essential that the seams between the planks be caulked. The relatively flexible caulking would ensure that the schooner would remain watertight even when her hull was pounded by the forces of wind and sea.

*Sultana* had over 3,000 feet of open, V-shaped seams on her bottom. The labor-intensive process that was used to caulk these seams was similar to what had been employed on the original schooner 230 years before. It began with cotton. Using a special mallet and an iron wedge, the crew hammered long

*Facing page: The vaulted shed under which* Sultana *was built was named in honor of Stig Torstenson and Donald Hewes, the project's two most dedicated volunteers. In this image,* Sultana *is less than six weeks away from being launched. The middle and upper rails have already been painted black and the upper portion of the hull has been coated with linseed oil and turpentine in preparation for the first coat of yellow ochre paint.*

The two Douglas fir tree trunks that would become Sultana's lower masts were custom cut in northern Oregon and then shipped across the country to Chestertown. It was shipwright A.J. Kolodziejski's job to turn them into finished spars.

In a feature rarely seen on modern vessels, **Sultana's** rudder passes through a hole in the bottom of the transom, up through the captain's cabin and then out through a hole in the aft end of the aftermost (poop) deck. The passageway for the rudder in the underside of the transom is seen here directly above shipwright Josh Herman's head.

Sultana's transom was the only portion of the vessel where extensive use was made of epoxy lamination. The rigidity of laminated cedar planks helps to add strength to the unsupported, overhanging transom without adding excess weight.

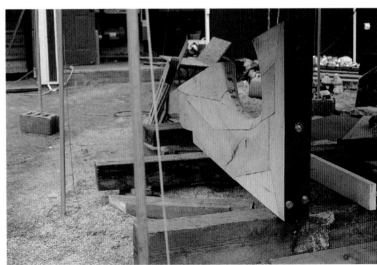

Sultana's 16-foot-tall, 2,000-pound rudder was pieced together from numerous timbers of oak and Osage. Unlike the original eighteenth-century rudder, the new rudder had to be shaped to accommodate a 32-inch-diameter propeller. The single piece of crooked Osage in the center of the rudder acts as the backbone onto which the other timbers are fastened.

strips of loosely spun cotton into the bottom of the seams. Special care was taken to put a kink into the cotton at intervals of about 1 inch along the entire length of each seam. These kinks prevented water from traveling through the cotton fibers lengthwise, just as a tight kink in a drinking straw prevents liquid from moving up or down the straw.

After each seam was stuffed with cotton, it was next caulked in a similar manner with an additional two layers of traditional ship's "oakum," which is made from tarred hemp or jute fibers loosely spun like cotton. Due to the coarser nature of these fibers, oakum tends to be larger than the cotton caulking material and is generally suitable for the wider portions of each seam. Altogether *Sultana*'s caulking required no less than one mile of cotton and almost two miles of oakum, all driven into each seam by hand.

To oversee the caulking John added an additional member to the professional shipyard crew, Mike Rodgers. Mike and his wife had recently come from Maine to purchase and rebuild an old Jim Richardson–built bugeye, *Jenny Norman*. While Mike worked on the bugeye, he was able to squeeze two days a week into his schedule to help with *Sultana*. Also taking a lead role in the caulking was volunteer Herb Wilkinson, who had caulked much of the deck and now dedicated his time exclusively to sealing up the bottom. Herb was the true hero of the caulking. It's a rare volunteer who is willing to spend three straight months (January, February, and March, no less!) crawling around underneath a schooner, iron and mallet in hand, driving in cotton and oakum week after week.

Amidst the rhythmic ringing of the caulking mallets, Stig and Donald built *Sultana*'s 16-foot-high, 1,000-pound rudder. The rudder was the last sizable piece of carpentry that absolutely had to be completed before launch. Six inches thick, the rudder was made up of eight interlocking timbers of oak and Osage held together by dozens of large bronze drift pins. The rudder was one of the rare items that required a significant deviation from *Sultana*'s original 1767 lines. For safety and practicality an engine had been included in the new *Sultana*, and in order to accommodate a propeller, a large elliptical notch was cut in the front edge of the rudder as well as in the back edge of the sternpost.

*In order to make* Sultana *watertight thousands upon thousands of feet of caulk were driven into the schooner's planking seams.* Sultana's *seams were caulked first with white, spun cotton and then recaulked a second and third time with traditional tarred brown oakum.*

*Volunteer Herb Wilkinson devoted over four months to caulking* Sultana's *hull and personally drove in more than a mile of cotton and oakum caulking.*

*The bottom of* Sultana's *bilge was sealed and leveled with roofing pitch in order to fill small cavities too low to be pumped dry by the schooner's bilge pumps. To lower the vessel's center of gravity two, 65-pound lead ballast weights were placed between each set of frames and then sealed in the pitch.*

Sultana's *brick fireplace was always a point of interest to shipyard visitors. Recreated directly from the original 1768 Royal Navy survey of* Sultana, *the masonry portion of the stove was built with handmade bricks composed of Chestertown clay and fired at Colonial Williamsburg. The iron chimney cap was custom made using hand-forged rivets. Historically the stove would have been used to heat the crew's food and warm the men. The masonry portion of the stove was done by Ray Cannetti, an experienced mason and stone carver, and Andrew Berry, chief of the brickyard at Colonial Williamsburg.*

Along with the modification of the rudder design Stig and Donald also had to fabricate templates for gudgeons and pintles—the fittings that would hinge the rudder to the sternpost of *Sultana.* To help with this task we were lucky to find Bob Mousley, the owner of Atlas Bronze in Philadelphia, one of a long line of foundry men dating back to the 1800s. Mousley's shop took the templates that Stig and Donald had made and used them to fashion wood and Styrofoam casting patterns for each gudgeon and pintle. From these patterns the custom bronze fittings for *Sultana*'s rudder were cast in much the same way comparable metal parts have been made for hundreds of years.

Because *Sultana* was to be launched with the assistance of a large crane it was logical as well as economical to plan to step the schooner's two masts and install the bowsprit on the day of the launch, while the crane was handy. Of course this plan could only be accomplished if the three spars were ready. Unfortunately by the middle of January, with only ten weeks to go, the two Douglas fir timbers from which the masts were to be hewn had yet to arrive from the West Coast. Our lumber broker in Oregon had obtained two trunks that would make perfect masts; the problem was finding a way to get them across the country.

In the fall of 2000 the price of diesel fuel had skyrocketed, driving many small shipping companies out of business. Simply finding a truck to drive two 62-foot trunks, each weighing 15,000 pounds, from Oregon to Maryland was proving to be next to impossible. Only after several months of diligent and at times frantic searching was a suitable truck located.

When the mast timbers finally arrived at the end of January, A.J. and several of the volunteers went straight to work cutting them down into their final shape. Most of the initial shaping was done with a large chain saw. First each trunk was cut down to a tapered square shape (they were cut to be 15 inches square on one end and 12 inches square on the other). Next the four sides were brought down to 8, then 16, and eventually 32 tapered angles. Finally the timbers were rounded off using a large wooden spar plane—similar to the type of tool that would have been used to fair *Sultana*'s original masts.

The entire process took about ten days for each mast and by the beginning of March most of the shaping was complete. The caulking was also finished at about the same time and so we were, by all estimates, in very good shape to launch in just over three weeks.

## The Final Weeks

In the original project plan created in 1997 John and I had scheduled *Sultana* to be ready almost two full months before the date of the launch. We did this guessing that the construction would encounter more than a few unexpected delays and that the finishing details would probably take longer than even our most cautious projections. As it turned out we had done somewhat better than we had anticipated. No doubt the final three weeks of work would be a blur of frenzied activity, but compared with what might have been it would at least be a reasonably controlled frenzy.

It was fortunate that we were on schedule because during those last weeks in March our days were filled with activities we hadn't anticipated in 1997. Though those of us working inside the shipyard gates had long been adjusting to the fact that *Sultana*'s construction was coming to an end, it seemed as if the rest of the world woke up one March morning and realized that we actually intended to put *Sultana* in the water. As launch day neared, people descended on the shipyard in ever-greater numbers telling us they needed to get one last look. We politely reminded them that *Sultana* wasn't going away, she was just going to move down the street a few hundred yards. This reassurance seemed to bring little solace to the citizens of Chestertown and beyond, who had grown attached to the idea of having a working shipyard in the middle of the town.

"You're going to build another one, aren't you?" many asked, both hopeful and worried.

Whatever else we had to do before putting *Sultana* in the water, taking these people on one last walk around the shipyard became a high priority for everyone. All of us—John, myself, the shipwrights, and the volunteers—took great satisfaction in the pleasure that *Sultana* was bringing to people. While in the larger sense we had built *Sultana* for the schoolchildren who would soon sail on her, in a more immediate sense, we had built her for the legions of people who had supported us and taken

*As much as possible* Sultana's *rig was prepared and assembled at the shipyard well before the launch. Items such as these grommetted hearts, shown here draped over the end of the bowsprit, were attached to the masts and spars so that the rig could be completed quickly once the vessel was in the water.*

*Using eighteenth-century techniques, a traditional wooden heart is spliced into the end of the forestay. A second identical heart is made fast to the end of the bowsprit and the two hearts are then connected with a rope lanyard. The lanyard makes three passes through each heart (hence the three groves) before it is tied off. In order to adjust the tension of the forestay the lanyard can be untied and either tightened or loosened.*

pleasure in the schooner's creation. If every one of them wanted to take one last look we felt obligated and gratified to spend as much time as it took to make that happen. It was the least we could do.

Painting *Sultana* took up most of the working hours that remained in the final weeks of construction. The topsides were painted according to colors described in the original logbooks: yellow ochre for the planks and black for the trim. The bottom was painted white to simulate the leaded tallow traditionally employed to retard marine growth on eighteenth-century sailing vessels. Much of the paint for *Sultana* was made and mixed by the Kirby Paint Company in New Bedford, Massachusetts. Kirby is a family business that has been mixing marine paint since before the Civil War and is still able to match eighteenth-century colors and finishes.

In the last days a lot of finishing details appeared on *Sultana*'s hull in a remarkably short time. Seacocks, chain plates, deadeyes, carvings, blown-glass windows, and more materialized as if by magic, though in truth their creation was the result of months, and in some cases years, of planning and work. In just a few days *Sultana* was transformed. Where there had been rough, unfinished planks, there was now a perfectly planed and painted surface displaying all the proper trimmings of an eighteenth-century schooner. For the first time *Sultana* took on the appearance of a finished vessel. She was ready to go.

## Moving Day

Moving *Sultana* was going to be a big deal. Looking back, if we had to do it all over again, I am certain we would search a little harder for a shipyard site closer to the water. But for *Sultana* this time, the trip to the river was certain to be exciting—a day we would all remember for the rest of our lives.

From a purely technical aspect, the move posed several challenges. First was *Sultana*'s size. The schooner's width mandated that we close the streets and clear cars from the planned

*Facing page: In order to legally carry passengers the new* Sultana *was equipped with a wide assortment of modern safety gear. Incorporating modern gear, such as the small life raft shown here, into* Sultana's *historic design was one of the most challenging aspects of the design process.*

*Sultana's deck was planked exclusively with Douglas fir from Washington State. Each plank measures 2¼ inches thick and 5 inches wide. Planks were fastened to the deck framing with double-wedged, black locust deck plugs.*

*The heart of* Sultana's *windlass is an octagonal cylinder of solid oak tapered at each end and weighing over 700 pounds. When weighing anchor the anchor cable is wrapped around the windlass cylinder and wooden "heavers" are inserted into the numerous square holes in order to gain leverage and spin the cylinder, thus raising the anchor. By employing the windlass a small number of crewmembers can lift several tons of weight.*

The evening before **Sultana** moved out of the shipyard, welder Martin Legg was hard at work attaching a restraining chain to **Sultana's** rudder. Working on an eighteenth-century schooner was a new experience for Martin, who lives in Rock Hall, Maryland, and specializes in fabricating oystering and clamming gear for Chesapeake watermen. Work on all parts of the vessel went on late into the night.

Thousands of people were expected in Chestertown to watch as **Sultana** was hauled down the main street to the waterfront. On the morning of moving day the shipyard volunteers donned neon-green vests and prepared for crowd control duty.

The shipyard crew worked furiously in the weeks leading up to Sultana's launch, making sure that every last detail was perfect. Here Josh Herman puts the finishing touches on **Sultana's** transom.

Sultana's original logbooks record the crew painting the vessel's hull on several occasions. According to the logs the sides were painted yellow ochre and the bends (trim) were coated with a black pitch and paint. With the help of several maritime historians, the correct ochre color was developed and custom produced for **Sultana** by the Kirby Paint Company in New Bedford, Massachusetts.

route. Her height, 18 feet from keel to rail, would force us to travel a circuitous path through Chestertown to avoid overhanging trees. In addition, it would be necessary to drop almost every power and telephone line in the town's central business district.

A second and more worrisome problem for the move was posed by the vessel's weight. Our best guess put *Sultana* at 100,000 to 120,000 pounds at the time of the launch. This would have been a minor concern if we'd been able to use a house-mover whose equipment could have spread the load widely over the surface of the street. Unfortunately, this was not an option. Standard house-moving equipment would have raised *Sultana*'s transom rail twenty-two feet off the road, higher than the main electrical cables that fed power to more than half the county. These cables were directly in the path of the move.

Employing a hydraulic trailer solved the height problem as such a trailer could carry *Sultana* with her rail at only nineteen feet over the street. However, in solving one problem we created another. Resting on the back of the trailer, all of *Sultana*'s weight would be placed directly over six closely spaced rubber tires. In turn these tires would transfer the load onto one small 8-by-11-foot section of roadway. There was concern that this might be more weight than some of Chestertown's three-hundred-year-old streets and storm drains could take. Lacking a better option we made an arrangement with the town, pledging to repair any damage we might cause to the streets. We crossed our fingers and hoped for the best.

Brownell Systems of Mattapoisett, Massachusetts, was hired to make the move. They were professionals and reputed to be the best in the business. It was comforting for us to know that the job did not require Brownell's biggest trailer, a huge 200-ton rig that had been employed during the launch of the schooner *Amistad* at Mystic Seaport. *Sultana* would ride instead on a similar but smaller 100-ton unit.

Tom Brownell and his team arrived in Chestertown, trailer and two truckloads of equipment in tow, on the afternoon of Thursday, March 22. For several days John and the volunteers had been preparing *Sultana* for loading. The scaffolding surrounding the schooner had been stripped away and the giant

*Sultana's transom includes four working windows (identifiable by the four swinging shutters or "deadlights") and one false decorative window in the center. Sultana's original plans show only the most basic lines of the transom and do not confirm or exclude the existence of windows. Windows were a popular feature in the transoms of many small American merchantmen of the period, and since Sultana's logbooks make several references to deadlights, the decision was made to include the windows on the transom.*

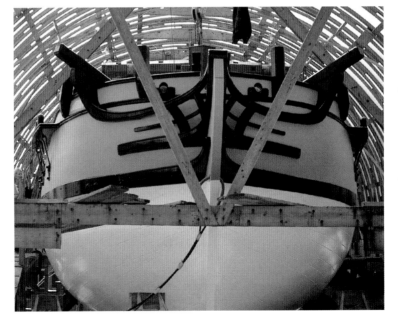

*The white paint on the underside of* Sultana's *hull was chosen to simulate the leaded tallow that was historically used to coat the bottom of sailing ships in the eighteenth century. The paint employed on* Sultana *is a modern antifouling paint designed to retard marine growth.*

*The day before* Sultana's *launch the schooner's two lower masts and bowsprit were hauled from the shipyard down to the Chestertown waterfront. Donald Hewes supplied the antique tractor and trailer rig from his Kent County farm.*

oak sleepers upon which she had sat for the last two and a half years were dragged out from underneath. Brownell's forked trailer was backed into the shed so the schooner's keel was positioned in the center. By 5 P.M. the preparations were complete and we handed *Sultana* over to Tom. For the next two days, until *Sultana* touched down in the Chester River, we would be little more than spectators.

Brownell wasted no time. *Sultana* was safely on the trailer within two hours of his arrival. There she would rest until morning when she would be hauled out of the shipyard and pulled down the street. We all went home to try to get a good night's sleep, suspecting that it might be our last for the rest of the weekend.

I arrived at the shipyard before dawn on the morning of the move thinking that I would be the first person on the scene. I was amazed to find that a small crowd had already gathered outside the yard's locked gate. I shouldn't have been surprised. Joyce, Michael, Faith, Kathy, and dozens of others had been hard at work for months planning the celebration for *Sultana*'s launch. Their effort had been just as intense as the work that had transpired at the shipyard. Television stations had been alerted, programs printed, dignitaries invited, and parties planned. Every hotel and motel room within seventy-five miles was booked. People were flying and driving into Chestertown from all across the country.

Within a few hours the crowd at the shipyard had grown to several thousand people. A look down the street revealed people standing on rooftops, hanging out of attic windows, and even sitting in the boughs and branches of trees, all to make certain they had a good spot from which to view the action. As we scanned the crowd, the most amazing thing to us was not its size, but rather that we recognized so many faces. This was no anonymous throng, come to gawk at the show and then disappear. These were friends and family, many of whom, even though they had never lifted a hammer or driven a trunnel, could take just as much satisfaction in *Sultana*'s creation as the shipwrights and volunteers.

At 9:00 A.M., almost as if on cue, a fleet of utility trucks rolled into town and spread out along the route of the move. Linemen in hard hats quickly scrambled up telephone poles and disconnected much of downtown's modern wiring. For a few hours Chestertown would be back in the eighteenth century.

After a final group picture in front of *Sultana* the shipyard was cleared and Brownell began his work. The powerful Volvo tractor rig attached to the front of the trailer roared to life, belching diesel exhaust high into the sky. The transmission was engaged, the pedal depressed, and after a few false starts, *Sultana* lurched forward, then slowly emerged from the protective shed where she had been built. As odd as it might sound this was the first time that John and the builders were able to see a full profile view of the schooner. Since the laying of the keel the building shed had made it impossible to have an unobstructed view of *Sultana*. As the schooner cleared the shed, we all had our first clear stem-to-stern look.

The only hitches in the move came early on as Brownell was hauling *Sultana* out of the shipyard and onto the street. First, because the path to the street was slightly uphill, the back tires of the tractor began to spin and dig their way down into the dirt surface of the yard. Fortunately Brownell was prepared—a second tractor rig had been brought down from Massachusetts for just such a possibility. The second rig was immediately put to work pulling the first tractor out of its rut.

The second hitch came as the rig made the 90-degree turn onto the street—the wheels of the trailer got hung up on the sidewalk. Again the second tractor came to the rescue, providing the necessary additional horsepower to haul the trailer's tires up and over the lip of the sidewalk, in the process crushing the 5-inch-thick, 3-foot-wide slab of concrete. Luckily this was the only damage that resulted from the move.

Once *Sultana* was safely clear of the shipyard the remainder of the trip went quickly—almost too fast—taking about as much time as a thoughtful stroll down to the river. The crowd walked along with the schooner as she moved, the entire procession stopping on a few occasions to allow for photographs or to wait for an errant wire to be lowered or removed. *Sultana* was safely at the river's edge well before noon, almost three hours earlier than we had estimated. All that remained was to wait patiently for the crane to arrive and lift *Sultana* into the river.

*Traffic was closed in downtown Chestertown for the best part of three days on launch weekend. Even parked cars had to be moved to make room for* Sultana's *masts as they made their way down to the water.*

*Volunteer Donald Hewes.*

According to Sultana's logbooks, it appears likely that her original Boston builders included a decorative figurehead on the bow of the vessel, but it was later removed by the Royal Navy. The new Sultana's figurehead (nicknamed Eileen, or "I-lean," because carver Jim Knowles often worked on her in the evenings at a Wilmington, Delaware, pub where he "leaned" her up against the bar) was created based upon the style popular in Boston in the mid-1700s. The figurehead represents a sultana, a member of a sultan's harem.

With only hours to go before moving **Sultana**, the shipyard volunteers remove a portion of the front of the boat shed to make way for the schooner to be pulled out.

## Arranging for *Keystone State*

That a crane would arrive to lift *Sultana* was still an issue in some doubt even as the schooner was making her way through the crowded, narrow streets of Chestertown toward her ultimate destination, the Chester River.

From the moment we decided to build *Sultana* in Chestertown it was obvious that a sizable crane would be required to get the schooner into the water. The search for a crane had begun within weeks of the laying of the keel. Early on, two suitable commercial barge cranes had been located on the Chesapeake. Both had the capacity to lift *Sultana* and both cost about $30,000 a day to hire! Upon hearing those quotes we took some time to regain our composure and then looked for a launching option more in keeping with our limited funding.

At the suggestion of Bob Bennett, one of *Sultana*'s "kitchen cabinet," we approached the United States Army to inquire if perhaps they could help us. Bob served on the board of directors of the Chesapeake Bay Maritime Museum in St. Michaels and had garnered the army's assistance a few years earlier to lift a historic bridge and bring it to the museum grounds.

The bridge lift had been done by the 949th Transportation Corps, a Baltimore-based army reserve group that had several cranes in its inventory and trained regularly to perform loading and salvage missions in time of war. Its regular schedule allowed time for "special missions" in order to provide its soldiers with unusual, real-life training scenarios. We were hoping that *Sultana* might qualify under that category.

Our contacts at the 949th were Colonel James Beirnes and CW4 Donald German. After we explained our situation they both agreed to see what they could do to help us get *Sultana* into the water. For almost a year the pair worked tirelessly to jump through the myriad of bureaucratic hoops required to gain approval for the mission. They even went so far as to arrange a "dry run" of the launch that brought a floating crane, three tugboats, and over sixty soldiers to Chestertown.

By Thanksgiving of 2000 it looked to be a done deal. The required paperwork had been signed, passed through the chain of command, and approved. It seemed certain that come March, the army would bring over its crane, pick up *Sultana*, and put

*The shaped and angled windows and the quarter badges on each side of* Sultana's *hull were recreated directly from the original 1768 Royal Navy survey.*

*When not under sail* Sultana *is powered by a 220-horsepower diesel engine that turns a 32-inch-diameter bronze propeller.*

*Drew McMullen looks on nervously on moving day, hoping that* Sultana's *weight won't crush the three-hundred-year-old streets of Chestertown.*

*The firm of Brownell Systems based in Mattapoisett, Massachusetts, was contracted to move* Sultana *from the shipyard to Chestertown's waterfront. Brownell employed a custom hydraulic trailer and a powerful diesel tractor rig to move the schooner.*

*Finding a crane of the size and capacity required to lift* Sultana's *weight was no easy task. In the end Uncle Sam came to* Sultana's *aid in the form of the U.S. Army Reserve 949th Transportation Company based in Baltimore, Maryland. The 949th operates the barge derrick* Keystone State, *the largest floating crane in the U.S. military's inventory. Rising over ten stories high, the giant crane dwarfed Chestertown's waterfront.*

her into the river—certain, that is, until we received a phone call from German one morning the following January.

"Drew, I'm calling because you might have already heard some of the rumors and I wanted to let you know that we're doing everything we can on this end to solve the problem." I had no idea what Don was talking about. "There might be an issue with the crane," he began.

The crane that was slated to help with *Sultana*'s launch was *Keystone State*, the first of a new class of mobile army cranes that had rolled off the production line only two years before. To date, three other identical cranes had been constructed and apparently an inherent design flaw was beginning to manifest itself in the course of normal operations. According to Don, in the last twelve months two other cranes of the same type as *Keystone State* had suffered "catastrophic" failures while being towed through relatively small seas. Both failures were related to the crane's control tower, which sat about a hundred feet off the barge's deck. Apparently, when the barge was being towed into an oncoming sea, the vibration created by the waves pounding on the bow was magnified as it made its way up to the control tower. By the time the vibration reached the top of the tower the steel beams and trusses were subjected to more than thirteen Gs of force, far more than they had been designed or built to withstand.

"So what you're telling me is the crane might not be able to help us with the launch?" I asked, just to make sure I knew exactly where we stood.

"For the time being *Keystone State* has been taken out of service by the army," Don responded. "It will take a special exemption from the highest levels at the Pentagon to do the launch, but I think we have a chance of getting one. The crane's welds have already been reinforced and on the northern Chesapeake we shouldn't have to worry about seas large enough to cause a problem."

German and Beirnes continued to work within army channels to get the launch mission reapproved. Within a few weeks a team of army engineers and inspectors was flown out from

*Facing page: Sultana's launch was one of the most exciting events in the three-hundred-year history of Chestertown. The Kent Community Marching Band opened the launch ceremony with a rousing parade down High Street.*

*It was a point of pride for all involved that* Sultana *would carry the name of Chestertown where she was built. Pres Harding crafted the schooner's hand-carved name boards. He is the grandson of Bronza Parks, one of the Chesapeake's most renowned builders of traditional wooden workboats.*

Michigan to examine the crane and determine its operational fitness. At the shipyard we nervously waited for the experts' opinion. There was now less than a month remaining before the launch and we had visions of a cast of thousands descending on Chestertown on the advertised date only to be disappointed when they found out that the launch had been canceled.

Colonel Beirnes called me from his cell phone as soon as the inspection verdict came in. "From an engineering standpoint the mission is a go," he began, much to my relief. "From here on in it's all political," he continued, my sense of relief evaporating as quickly as it had appeared. "We've taken away the easy reason to say no to this mission; now we have to convince the powers that be that there's a worthwhile reason for saying yes."

Our efforts to get the politicians to say yes were dealt a significant setback by a tragic event that took place halfway around the globe. On the morning of Sunday, February 9, the nuclear submarine USS *Greeneville* collided with a Japanese fishing trawler, sending the trawler and nine of those on board to the bottom of the Pacific ocean. At the time of the collision *Greeneville* had been giving a special tour to a group of civilian VIPs. In the uproar following the collision the propriety of mixing complex military operations with civilian personnel was closely scrutinized both in Washington and in the national media. This only served to make our case for the army's involvement in *Sultana*'s launch that much more difficult.

To his credit Colonel Beirnes persisted in his efforts to gain approval for the launch mission even when all indications suggested it was a lost cause. With less than a week to go we were frantically making arrangements for an alternative crane and scrambling to find a sponsor to foot the bill. Finally when it looked as if we had just about run out of options with the army, Colonel Beirnes decided he simply wouldn't take no for an answer. At a moment's notice he boarded a plane and flew to Atlanta, the home of the United States Army Reserve Command where the *Sultana* mission application was frozen

*Joyce Huber Smith and captain-to-be Gioia Blix look on in awe as the schooner is lifted into the air.*

*Alexandra Conran, the shipyard's youngest volunteer, was given the honor of christening* Sultana *on the day of the launch.*

Facing page: Sultana *sat quietly at the foot of High Street for a full day prior to her launch. Throughout the day and long into the evening the schooner was surrounded by people getting their last glimpse before she went into the water.*

in bureaucratic limbo. If someone was going to say no to the mission they would have to say it to the colonel's face.

Ultimately the determination of Colonel Beirnes and CW4 German, as well as a good word from local Congressman Wayne Gilchrest, paid off. With only seventy-two hours to spare the mission was given final approval by Army Command. The only condition placed on the operation was that the wind be no higher than 15 knots at the time *Keystone State* moved across the Bay from Baltimore.

Walking alongside *Sultana* as the Brownell trailer carried her through the streets of Chestertown, I kept one eye closely trained on the surface of the street with the expectation that at any minute it might buckle under *Sultana*'s great weight. The other eye I directed toward the treetops, which, to everyone's alarm, were swaying back and forth from a stiff southwest wind. According to the weather report the wind on the Bay was gusting to 25 knots, 10 knots higher than the limit stipulated by the army engineers. We had been trying unsuccessfully all morning to raise German on board *Keystone State* to see if the mission had been scrubbed. Finally, shortly after *Sultana*'s arrival at the river's edge, we received word that *Keystone State* had left Baltimore and was now making her way into the mouth of the Chester River. By late afternoon the army rig had motored all the way up to Chestertown and tied up alongside the town wharf. The final piece was now in place.

## The Big Lift

A crowd numbering nearly ten thousand people assembled along the Chestertown waterfront on the morning of March 24, 2001. The town's small streets were brimming with people and virtually every window, porch, and rooftop with a view of the action was filled to capacity. The Chester River bridge, just upriver from the launch area, was lined with spectators almost all the way across to the opposite shore. In the harbor a swarm of boats, canoes, and kayaks milled about restlessly awaiting the big lift.

Facing page: Sultana's *hull creaked initially as she was lifted off the Brownell trailer and into the air. Once airborne, however, the remainder of* Sultana's *flight was remarkably peaceful and quiet.*

*Sultana*'s midmorning launch was preceded by a short ceremony that included remarks from the mayor, several dignitaries, and, of course, John Swain. For those of us who had been directly involved with *Sultana*'s construction it was especially gratifying to see and hear John address the crowd from the speaker's podium. For the best part of four years John had been the glue that held *Sultana* and the shipyard together. Through his work, determination, generosity, ingenuity, caring, and kindness, John had singlehandedly set the tone that made his dream of *Sultana* a reality. Listening to John address the assembled crowd it was comforting to think that his dedication had been rewarded.

The final official act before the launch was the christening. In a flash of inspiration Joyce had suggested that Aly, *Sultana*'s youngest volunteer, break the bottle of champagne across the schooner's stem and send her on her way. Nothing could have been more appropriate. For three years Aly, now ten years old, had been one of *Sultana*'s most dedicated and enthusiastic supporters. In all likelihood at some (hopefully distant) point in the future Aly will be the last person left from our shipyard family. If *Sultana* is our gift to the future, a source of inspiration and learning that will endure long after those of us who created her are gone, then Aly is our ambassador. Seeing her, dressed in her Sunday best, break the champagne bottle across *Sultana*'s bow we knew there was no one better for the job.

With Aly's work complete the last thing to do was to put *Sultana* into the water. During the ceremony Brownell and the army crew fitted a large lifting harness under and around *Sultana*'s hull. The harness was composed of four wide fabric straps shackled to two steel lifting bars. The lifting bars were in turn connected on each end to a four-point cable bridle that led to a single lifting loop where the crane's hook was attached. At the conclusion of the ceremony, and only after triple-checking each connection, Brownell gave the signal to the crane operator and the lift began.

*John Swain looks on as four years of his life's work comes to fruition.*

Facing page: *Tension eased and excitement built as* Sultana *was lowered toward the surface of the Chester River. A great cheer was heard from the crowd as the schooner's keel broke the surface of the water.*

Once **Sultana** was floating free in the water the crew's first task was to make certain that she wasn't sinking. It is natural for a new wooden hull to leak the first time it is put in the water. It took almost a month for the schooner's wooden planks to swell to the point where she was watertight.

*After years of hard work the building crew experienced a profound sense of satisfaction standing on the decks of the vessel as she floated for the first time in the Chester River.*

*Sultana's foremast is slipped though a hole in the deck and then lowered down into place. Eight Osage wedges were used to secure the mast where it passed through the deck.*

*While the giant army crane was still handy, **Sultana's** two masts and bowsprit were lifted and fitted into place. Here the crew works to slide the bowsprit into a slot in the bow of the vessel.*

Slowly the giant cable winch on the barge began to take up slack. Within a few minutes the straps of the lifting harness were pulled taut around the schooner's belly. The thick white oak planks of *Sultana*'s hull creaked in protest as the weight of the schooner was gradually transferred from the trailer supports to the lifting harness and crane. Then came a loud "pop" as a support pad on the trailer, deprived of its load, detached and fell away from the schooner's hull. Several similar "pops" followed in rapid succession until *Sultana* was raised free from the trailer's cradle and began her short flight to the river.

Watching *Sultana* slowly "drift" through the air was a surreal experience. The lifting power of *Keystone State* was more than a match for the schooner's weight. *Sultana* seemed to move almost without effort—as if she were being levitated, not simply lifted. There was no roar of straining engines, no heated commands from the army crew, just a perfectly shaped, freshly painted hull quietly floating against the backdrop of puffy white clouds and a cobalt blue sky.

If there was an exception to the general sense of calm, it was to be found in the face of Tom Brownell. Tom had designed and built the lifting harness and it would be his head on the chopping block if anything went wrong. The visible tension in Tom's face eased somewhat as *Sultana* swung out over the water but was only erased completely when the schooner made her descent toward the water and her white keel was finally enveloped by the waters of the Chester River.

A huge cheer went up from the crowd when *Sultana* touched the water. A chorus of boat horns filled the harbor and the sound of cannon fire erupted from the shore. A great rush of exhilaration, relief, and, finally, pent-up exhaustion swept over all involved. We had done it. What had started as an idea in one man's head was now, after four years and almost two hundred thousand man-hours of work, a reality, floating in the river before our eyes. After over two hundred years of confinement on a sheet of paper in a London filing cabinet, *Sultana* was finally back in the water where she belonged.

# Chapter 12

# November 1772: *Sultana* Returns to England

With just six months gone 1772 had already been hard on *Sultana.* The schooner began the new year trapped in thick ice just south of Philadelphia. Unable to break free to resume her patrols until March, *Sultana* suffered the loss of her mainmast when it snapped in a gale on the twenty-second of that month. April and May saw the schooner's men board and rummage dozens of vessels on the lower Delaware River. In contrast with previous years Inglis noted with concern that the Americans had grown significantly more brazen in their resistance. Increasingly *Sultana* was forced to bring her guns to bear *and* to fire them in order to make American merchant vessels heave to and submit—a distressing sign of things to come. *Sultana* engaged in her first full-scale firefight on May 9 when the men of the brig *Carolina* narrowly failed in an attempt to retake their recently seized vessel by force. Later that same week one of *Sultana's* sailors, Henry Black, was lost overboard while boarding another American vessel.[1]

*Sultana* and her men were being stretched to their limits. This small schooner, built initially as a private yacht and then refitted as a revenue schooner for the Royal Navy, was now being called upon to engage in regular armed combat. With her small size and limited armament, it was a mission for which she was ill suited. The more the Americans became aware of *Sultana's* shortcomings, the more they were inclined to test them. As a result Inglis's position grew increasingly difficult

with each passing week. With the arrival of the latest news from Rhode Island, it was clear that *Sultana's* situation would only get worse.

Inglis had never been particularly fond of Lieutenant William Dudingston, the commander of *Sultana's* sister ship HMS *Gaspee,* an armed revenue schooner that generally patrolled the waters off Rhode Island. To Inglis's thinking the overzealous and haughty manner with which Dudingston discharged his duties only served to unnecessarily antagonize the colonists, in the process making the job of the other captains in the fleet that much more difficult. Indeed, to the Royal Navy's detriment, Dudingston and *Gaspee* were infamous throughout North America as symbols of British tyranny and oppression.

Despite his feelings for Dudingston, Inglis was horrified to learn that the lieutenant had been shot and HMS *Gaspee* burned by rebellious Rhode Islanders on June 9. If a similar incident involving the French or Spanish had occurred, Inglis would be among the first clamoring for a declaration of war. The details of the notorious events as they were related to Inglis were these. Apparently a group of rebellious Rhode Islanders, eager to get Dudingston ashore where they could work him over at their leisure, laid a trap for HMS *Gaspee.* The bait was the small packet boat *Hannah,* en route from Newport to Providence. By design *Hannah's* captain sailed his vessel deliberately under the nose of the revenue schooner. Dudingston took the bait, and, when *Hannah* refused to heave to as ordered, he gave orders to pursue the smaller vessel into the shallows around Namquit Point, just south of Providence. There *Gaspee* soon found herself hard aground and surrounded by boatloads of angry colonists. Dudingston had barely given the order for the colonists to disperse when a hail of gunfire knocked him to the deck, wounded in both the arm and the groin. Within a few minutes the rebels had overwhelmed *Gaspee*'s crew and set the schooner aflame.[2]

*Gaspee*'s demise, not to mention the method by which it had been effected, was a piece of black news for all of His Majesty's revenue schooners, including *Sultana*. Especially worrisome was the fact that the perpetrators had so easily disappeared among the local population. With so many witnesses the absence of a single individual willing to step forward and identify the rebels spoke volumes about the disposition of the Rhode Islanders toward the Crown.

Back in Boston at the headquarters of the Royal Navy's North American Squadron, the admirals contemplated what steps to take in response to the burning of *Gaspee*. The almost decade-old policy of naval enforcement in Britain's North American colonies had nearly run its course. Though there had been several tactical victories since the first revenue cutters had been put into service back in 1764, in a strategic sense the British policy had been an undeniable failure. Just as the Crown's most intractable opponents had so often claimed, the cost of maintaining the navy schooners in North America far exceeded the revenue they produced in the course of their duties. Not only had the British Parliament and Navy enraged the colonists through the imposition and enforcement of the Stamp and Townshend Acts, they had put themselves further into debt while doing it! Tragically a policy that had been conceived in order to strengthen the bonds between the colonies and the mother country (while producing a much-needed source of revenue to boot) had succeeded brilliantly in producing exactly the opposite result. Whether the admirals were ready to admit it or not, the era when the British Navy could dictate the course of events along the coast of North America was quickly coming to a close.

This 1765 painting of the schooner **Baltick** *is perhaps the most detailed contemporary rendering of a small American-built square-topsail schooner under sail.* Sultana *would have looked quite similar to* Baltick *as she patrolled the coast of colonial North America. Photograph courtesy Peabody Essex Museum (M2367/negative no. 11749).*

Within a few weeks of *Gaspee*'s burning, Inglis received orders from the Admiralty to take *Sultana* off her station on the Delaware and proceed directly to Boston. Departing from Chester Town on the Delaware on September 1, *Sultana* made her way down river and passed Cape May on the third, then turned north and passed Montauk Point on the fourth, Nantucket shoals on the fifth, Cape Cod on the seventh, and finally arrived in Boston Harbor on the morning of September 9.[3]

After *Sultana* waited a month at anchor in Boston, the Admiralty finally decided that the time had come to relieve the schooner from her duties in North America. In the days ahead larger ships and more powerful guns would be needed to deal with the rebellious colonists. The navy no longer had a use for a vessel of *Sultana*'s small size and extremely limited firepower. Orders were issued for Inglis and the schooner to depart at once for England where the ultimate fate of the schooner would be decided.

On the morning of October 11 HMS *Sultana* weighed anchor in North America for the last time. Once the anchor was pulled clear and seized to the cathead Inglis ordered the men to set the schooner's topsails and instructed Bruce to steer *Sultana* out into the open waters of the North Atlantic. On the evening of October 12, *Sultana* passed just northeast of the tip of Cape Cod—the last point of land her crew would see before arriving in England. Though he could not know it at the time, as the sun set that evening Inglis was taking his last look at the continent of North America. Inglis would live to an advanced age but the events of the coming American Revolution would make him forever a stranger to the land of his birth.[4]

After a harrowing crossing of the Atlantic, *Sultana* arrived in England on November 22, 1772. Inglis, Bruce, and the crew stayed with the schooner until December 7, when they were paid off and *Sultana* was officially taken out of active service. Having no need for a vessel of *Sultana*'s size the Royal Navy promptly sold the schooner at a public auction for a selling price of eighty-five pounds. From the date of her sale, no records of *Sultana*'s activities or whereabouts have been found, and her ultimate fate remains a mystery to this day.[5]

John Inglis went on to have a long and distinguished career with the Royal Navy, ultimately retiring as a vice admiral in 1805. As mentioned Inglis never again returned to the shores of North America, nor did he again see his brother Samuel who became an ardent patriot for the American cause. In contrast John Inglis remained a devout Tory for the rest of his days. He died in 1807 at Redhall, his family's ancestral estate in Scotland. Descendants of the Inglis line can be found today, both in Scotland and in the Americas.[6]

*Chapter*
*13*

# 2001: *Sultana* Tests Her Sails

It took almost two weeks for the shipyard crew to recover from the launch. For the first few days we all walked around in a virtual stupor, as if we'd just survived an earthquake and were still adjusting to the radically transformed landscape. The shipyard was empty without *Sultana* and, as counterintuitive as it might sound, the schooner looked strangely out of place floating in the river.

This communal sense of dislocation gradually evaporated as we grasped both the enormity of the work that lay before us and the short amount of time we had to complete it. "The last 10 percent of the job is 90 percent of the job," someone once said. I don't know to whom this quote is attributed (perhaps Yogi Berra) but clearly there is some truth to it. Belowdecks *Sultana* was still an empty shell. Above decks we had managed to step the two lower masts and secure the bowsprit on the day of the launch but we still had to run almost two miles of rigging.

For the first time since the laying of the keel there was a sense of nervous urgency to the work, a feeling that if we didn't give it our all every minute of every hour we might not finish on time. People who had already been giving 100 percent now began to give 150 percent. Volunteers who had been coming one day a week now came three, and those who had been coming three came five!

The extra effort quickly bore fruit. Cabins and bunks materialized belowdecks in rapid succession. The complexity of the rig multiplied daily as spars, sails, halyards, and sheets were added. The mechanics got the engine running and the electricians wired the hull. Though she was still a long way from completion, by the middle of May *Sultana* was ready for her first sail.

Just before the launch we had made a significant addition to the *Sultana* team. Gioia Blix was named to be *Sultana*'s first captain. While we had been building *Sultana*, Gioia had been busy captaining the sloop *Clearwater* on the waters of New York's Hudson River. Like *Sultana, Clearwater* is an educational vessel, and, also like *Sultana, Clearwater* is steered with a tiller. These factors, plus Gioia's professionalism, quiet confidence, and firm yet easygoing manner, made her the clear choice to be the first to take command of *Sultana.*

During the second half of May, Gioia, the shipwrights, and the volunteers took the schooner through her initial sea trials. At first, *Sultana* was limited to sailing under the power of only one of her six sails. Week by week additional sails were tested as Mark Roesner and the rigging crew readied them. By Memorial Day all four lower sails —the two jibs, the foresail, and the mainsail—had been raised and successfully handled in light air. A few free hours and a stiff breeze would give us a chance to see what *Sultana* could really do.

The magic moment came on the afternoon of May 30, 2001. A moderately strong cold front had swooped down from Canada

124   Schooner *Sultana*

the previous evening and by midmorning the wind on the river was blowing a steady 15 to 20 knots out of the northwest. Still under the gun to complete construction the crew worked diligently through the day at their appointed tasks, hoping that the wind would hold until after work when *Sultana* and they would be free for a sail. At 4 P.M. the wind was still a steady 15 knots and the crew excitedly put down their tools and cleared the decks, readying the schooner for "sea."

Apparently word had gotten around town that we were going to raise sail that afternoon. By the time we were ready to cast off, the end of the town dock was crowded with people, some looking to hitch a ride, others just hoping to catch a glimpse of *Sultana* under sail. With a full load of passengers and crew we cast off the dock lines and motored a short distance upriver until the schooner sat directly in front of Chestertown. There the captain took *Sultana*'s bow up into the wind and ordered the crew to raise sail.

The inner jib and the mainsail were the first to be set. The makeshift crew worked hard to raise the sails smartly and efficiently, hoping perhaps to do right in the eyes of *Sultana*'s original crew from two centuries before. Once the main and the jib were up the captain ordered the helmsman to take the schooner off the wind and make way down the river. As the schooner turned, the jib and the main filled with wind and *Sultana* heeled noticeably to port. In less than a minute she was doing a respectable 4 knots. Thus far we liked the way she was sailing and everyone was eager to raise more canvas and see what we could squeeze out of her.

About a mile downriver from Chestertown the river makes a sharp turn to the southeast and then runs straight in that direction another two miles. This long open fetch is perfect for sailing in a northwest wind and we knew this would be the place to test the schooner's sailing capability. Just before reaching the bend the foresail was eased out until it caught wind and filled like a parachute. For the second time *Sultana* heeled

Facing page: Sultana's *first sail was truly a magical moment for the shipwrights and volunteers, many of whom had been involved with the project for over four years and had helped to fell the trees from which she was built.*

*Rigger Mark Roesner straddles* Sultana's *forestay as he "hanks on" the schooner's jib.*

*The first time* Sultana's *sails were raised was a thrill for everyone on the building crew—even though they were raised while the schooner was securely fastened to the dock.*

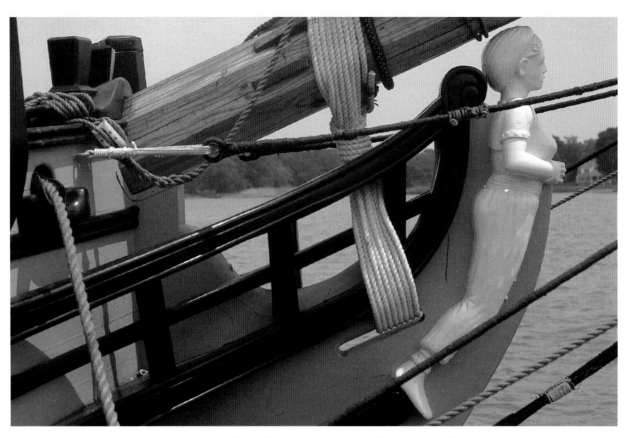

Sultana's bowsprit is lashed to a slot in the billethead in order to keep it stable as the vessel sails.

Sultana's rig contains none of the mechanical components, such as shackles or turnbuckles, found on a modern sailing craft. Every rigging attachment, every block, every shroud, and every halyard was secured with time-consuming hand lashings.

For her launch Sultana had been stripped clean of gear and equipment in order to reduce her weight. Once she was in the water, equipment (including her four 150-pound swivel guns) was quickly added to the schooner.

*After a successful first sail,* Sultana *and her crew motor home to Chestertown.*

*On deck one of* **Sultana**'s *most distinctive features is her 7-foot-long steering tiller. After a few outings a block and tackle was added to the tiller to assist with the steering.*

Sultana's *first sea trials took place in mid-May 2001, almost a month before her professional crew was scheduled to arrive. During the trials the shipwrights and volunteers, only a few of whom had experience sailing traditional schooners, served with distinction as* Sultana's *first sailing crew.*

*Volunteer Dave Roberts works to finish a detail on* Sultana's *railing.*

Sultana's *mainsail is lashed to a series of large oak mast hoops, which slide up the greased sides of the mainmast when the sail is raised.*

noticeably to port until her ballast took hold and the force of the wind was translated into forward motion.

After *Sultana* rounded the bend, the windward shore receded behind us and the wind speed began to increase steadily. Now sailing on a broad reach the schooner rapidly picked up speed, first to 5 knots, then to 6, and eventually to 7 knots. Though this might not sound like much to those accustomed to traveling 70 miles an hour on the highway, I assure you that on an 80-ton schooner sailing between the tree-lined banks of a narrow, bending river like the Chester, 7 knots felt a bit like riding a freight train through the bottom of a short narrow canyon. It was pretty amazing.

Unfortunately our sail was over almost as soon as it had begun. Traveling at that speed we reached the end of the fetch in just a few minutes and were forced to strike sail. It had been a short trip, and by no means perfect, but for many of us on board, it was the most exciting and satisfying few minutes we had ever spent on the water.

Walking off the dock that evening I stopped for a moment to look back at *Sultana*, her sails tightly furled and the top half of her rig illuminated by the glow of the setting sun. Riding next to her at the new town dock, not entirely by coincidence, were my old friends *Elsworth* and *Annie D*. Thanks to the mayor and the council of Chestertown, these three proud vessels will share a home on the town's waterfront for the foreseeable future. Seeing the three wooden vessels riding there together was almost like looking at a snapshot of the last ten years of my life. I felt incredibly fortunate to have come to Chestertown to work alongside John, Joyce, Michael, and all the other incredible people who gave their all to turn the dream of *Sultana* into a reality.

*Sultana's completed rig contains no fewer than eighty different sail controls. The process of learning where each line leads and what it does could take a seaman several weeks and indeed it is from this process that the saying "learning the ropes" is derived.*

*Each of* Sultana's *two lower masts is supported by eight wires, or shrouds. The end of each shroud is seized around a round, three-holed deadeye. This deadeye is linked by rope to a similar deadeye fastened by an iron band to the side of the hull. The rope lanyard can be tightened or loosened to adjust the tension of the rig.*

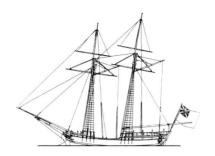

# Specifications: *Sultana* 2001

Sparred length, 97'
LOA (length overall), 59'
LOD (length on deck), 52'
LWL (length waterline), 51' 3"
Length between perpendiculars
  (range of the deck), 50' 6"
Draft, 8'
Beam, 16' 8"
Height of rig, 67'

Sail area, 1,830 square feet
  excluding main topsail and fore course
Mainmast (heel to cap), 54' 4"
Main boom, 37' 3"
Main gaff, 17' 6"
Main topmast, overall, 26'
Main yard, 28'
Main topsail yard, 20'
Bowsprit, 27' 8", outboard, 21'

Jib boom, overall, 21' 2"
Foremast (heel to cap), 51' 3"
Fore topmast, overall, 24'
Fore gaff, 15'
Fore yard, 28' 6"
Fore topsail yard, 20' 10"
Weight, 68.05 long tons
  (152,432 pounds)
Power, 225 hp diesel

---

Keel
  White oak *(Quercus alba)*, locally selected, cut, and milled, 40' 3" in length, sided 12", molded forward 18", aft 12"
Ballast
  Outside: 10,500 pounds, cast in two 5,250-pound sections and scarfed together
  Inside: 35,000 pounds, lead ingots approximately 65 pounds each secured to the hull with stainless steel strapping fastened to the keelson and frames
Stem
  Osage orange *(Maclura pomifera)*, all locally selected, cut, and milled, sided 10", molded 12", fastened with ⅝" silica bronze rod, nuts, washers, and clinch rings
Sternpost
  Osage orange, sided 10"; 16" fore-and-aft siding at heel, fastened with ⅝" silica bronze rod, nuts, washers, and clinch rings

Stemson knee (deadwood)
  Osage orange, fore-and-aft length of 11' with vertical rise of 5', sided 10", fastened with ⅝" silica bronze rod, nuts, washers, and clinch rings
Frames
  Osage orange, thirty-nine frames, with 16-inch "timber and space" (8"-wide frames with 8" space between). Fastened with ⅝" silica bronze carriage bolts at futtock butts and with 1" Osage trunnels between the butts. Average 8–10 futtocks per frame.
Keelson
  White oak, sided 10", molded 10". Two pieces with 4' hook scarf. Scarf fastened with eight ⅝" silica bronze carriage bolts.
Keelson, frame, keel fastening
  Two ¾" silica bronze bolts pass through the keelson, floors, keel, and ballast at each frame. Each bolt is approximately 3' in length with nuts and washers on each end.

Garboard
> White oak 3" thick fastened with two ½" silica bronze lag bolts at each frame and edge-bolted through the keel with ½" silica bronze carriage bolts between the frames

Planking
> White oak, 2½" thick, average 8" in width, from stock 18' to 30' in length. Fastened with two ½" silica bronze lag bolts at each butt and with two 1" wedged Osage trunnels at each frame between the butts.

Wale strake
> White oak, 3½" by 8" with two scarfs per side. Fastened with two ⅝" silica bronze carriage bolts at each frame.

Deck beams
> Main deck beams: Osage orange, sided 9" and molded 7"
> Foredeck beams: Osage orange, sided 9" and molded 5"
> Quarterdeck beams: Osage orange, sided 5" and molded 5"
> Beams fastened with ½" and ⅝" silica bronze rod and 1" Osage trunnels

Transom
> Osage orange framed, white cedar (Chamaecyparis thyoides) planked.

Knees
> 36 lodging knees, 24 hanging knees, hackmatack (tamarack, Larix laricina), 4" to 6" sided, 16" to 27" arm, 18" to 30" body, each fastened with four to six ⅝" silica bronze drift pins with clinch rings

Clamps
> Deck clamps: white oak, 4" by 6"
> Bilge clamps: white oak, two 4" by 6", scarfed and bolted
> Both clamps fastened with one ⅝" silica bronze carriage bolt and one 1" trunnel at each frame

Ceiling
> White oak, 2" thick, average 8" in width. Fastened with two ½" silica bronze lag bolts at each butt and two 1" wedged Osage trunnels at each frame between the butts.

Decking
> Quarter-sawn Douglas fir (Pseudotsuga menziesii), 2¼" by 5". Fastened with one 5/16" silica bronze lag bolt at each end and one 1" double-wedged locust (Robinia pseudoacacia) trunnel at each deck beam between the ends. There are no butt joints in the deck.

Collision bulkhead
> Two opposing diagonal layers of 1½" white cedar, laminated and fastened to an Osage frame

Engine room bulkheads
> White oak, 3" thick fastened with ⅝" silica bronze rod

Sealants, preservatives, and paint
> Roofing tar (used as bedding compound between all adjoining wood surfaces)
> Copper bottom paint (used for priming all adjoining wood surfaces)
> Pine tar, linseed oil, turpentine, Japan drier
> Sodium borate (antifungal compound used in a dissolved solution)
> Kirby Marine Paint

Caulking
> Planking below the wale: primer paint, cotton, oakum, Interlux brown seam compound
> Planking above the wale: Sikaflex primer, cotton, oakum, Sikaflex 240
> Decking: Sikaflex primer, cotton, Sikaflex 290 DC

Waterways
> Osage orange, 4" sided, 5" molded

Scuppers
> Lead lined, lead fastened with ¾" silica bronze ring nails

Channels
> White oak, through-bolted with ⅝" rod through the deck clamp. Clinch ring used on interior of deck clamp and nut/washer used on outside.

Chain plates
> Hand-forged, hot-rolled steel, 2" by ½", with preventer links. Fastened to hull with two ¾" hand-forged, hot-rolled steel bolts through the frames and ceiling and secured with wedges and plates. All steel hot-dipped galvanized.

Catheads
> Osage orange hewn from natural crooks. Fastened with ⅝" silica bronze rod.

Windlass
> White oak, 15½" by 10' with inlaid Osage bearing surfaces. Posts fashioned from white oak and Osage orange.

Windlass heavers
> White oak and Osage orange

Rudder
> Osage orange, 6" stock with white oak filler. Fastened with ⅝" silica bronze rod and clinch rings. Head of the rudder is encapsulated in a hot-dipped galvanized, hot-rolled steel cap.

Gudgeons and pintles
> Custom cast-aluminum bronze fastened with silica bronze wood screws and ½" silica bronze lag bolts. Pintle diameter 1½".

Tiller
> Osage orange passing through the head of the rudder and secured with an Osage wedge

Hatches
> Coamings: Osage orange, fastened through the deck beams with ⅝" silica bronze rods and clinch rings.
> Grates: white oak, 2" thick
> Hatch covers: red cedar (Thuja plicata), canvas-covered and painted

Interior partitions
> 1" by 6" tongue-and-groove red cedar on white oak framing

Cabin sole
> Officer's quarters and galley: Douglas fir fastened and caulked as the weather decks
> Main hold: white oak, laid edge to edge

Ship's stove, masonry portion

Hand-fashioned bricks, 9" by 4" by 3", made from Chestertown clay.

Traditional lime mortar. Seated on a bedded sheet of stainless steel.

Ship's stove, iron chimney

Interior surface: welded stainless steel

Exterior surface: hot-rolled steel sheets with hand-forged rivets, corner brackets, and hardware

Insulation: high-temperature insulation between exterior and interior surfaces

Fastening: chimney is secured at each corner to cabin sole beams with four, 3' hooked steel rods secured with nuts and washers beneath the beams

Masts and spars

Main and foremast: Douglas fir, 14" maximum diameter cut from trees 30" by 61'

Mast steps: Osage orange fastened to the keelson and frames with ⅝" silica bronze rod

Yards, gaffs, topmasts, jib boom and boom: Douglas fir laminated hollow

Bowsprit: Douglas fir

Sails and rigging

Standing rigging: ⅝" galvanized wire rope, parceled and served. Three-strand Dacron for lanyards and lashings.

Running rigging: ½" to ⅞" diameter Roblon

Blocks: Ash bodies with self-lubricating bronze sheaves, rope stropping

Cleats: Osage orange made on site

Sails: Oceanus cloth with Buff Polyester hand-sewn boltropes and cringles. Bronze grommets.

Auxiliary propulsion

Engine: John Deere 6068 turbo diesel, 225 horsepower

Transmission: Twin disc 3:1 reduction gear

Mounts: solid mounted

Shaft: 2" diameter Aquamet 22 shaft, housed in fiberglass shaft tube with cutless bearings at each end, engine-cooling water introduced at the stuffing box and pumped out through the shaft tube

Prop: right-hand, three-bladed, 32" diameter, 28" pitch

Exhaust system

Stainless steel, 4" diameter with applied, high-temperature ceramic insulation and insulation blanket. Dry exhaust from engine to top of loop under deck where engine-cooling water is introduced. Exhaust/cooling water enters water-lift muffler prior to discharge overboard.

Armament

Four half-pound swivel guns with hand-forged, hot-rolled steel yokes and monkey tails.

Windows

Single pane windows, safety laminated from two ¼" panes of hand-blown glass

Systems

Electric: 12 volt, 110 AC inverter, shore power

Lighting: hand-made reproduction ship's lanterns with mica lenses

Waste management: Lavac head system with 110-gallon holding tank

Fuel tanks: two 120-gallon aluminum tanks with baffles

Lightning protection: Lightning rods on each topmast wired to 4' by 8' copper plate secured to the bottom of the hull.

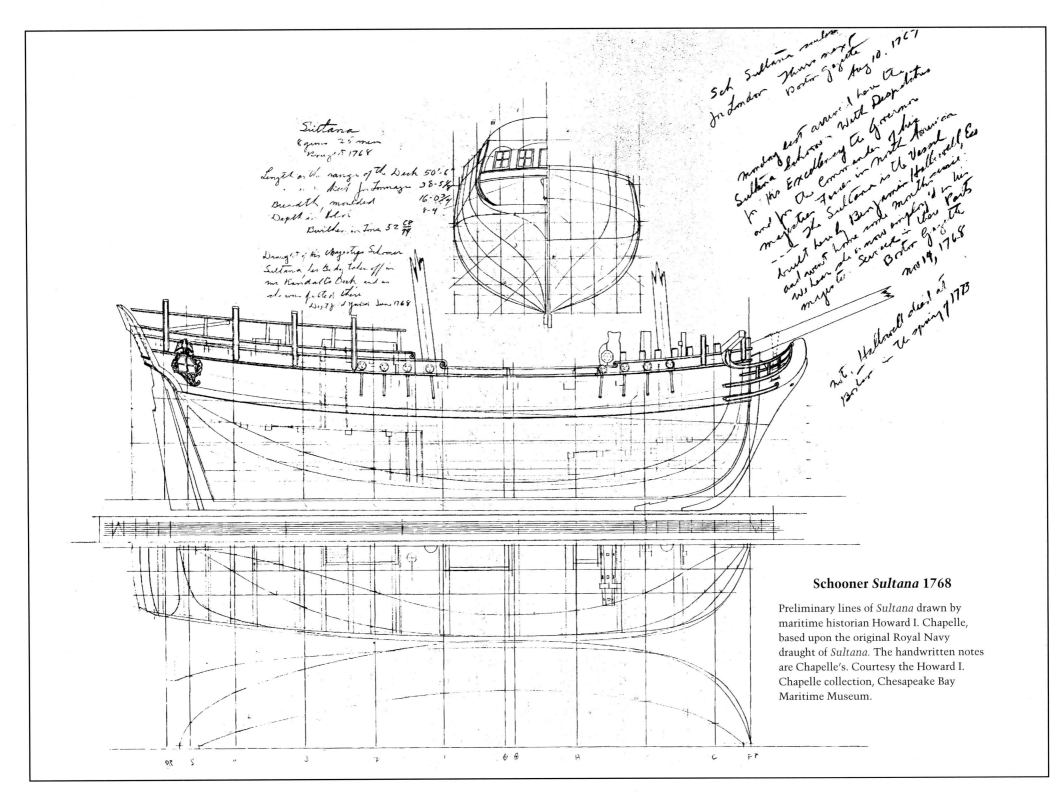

**Schooner *Sultana* 1768**

Preliminary lines of *Sultana* drawn by maritime historian Howard I. Chapelle, based upon the original Royal Navy draught of *Sultana*. The handwritten notes are Chapelle's. Courtesy the Howard I. Chapelle collection, Chesapeake Bay Maritime Museum.

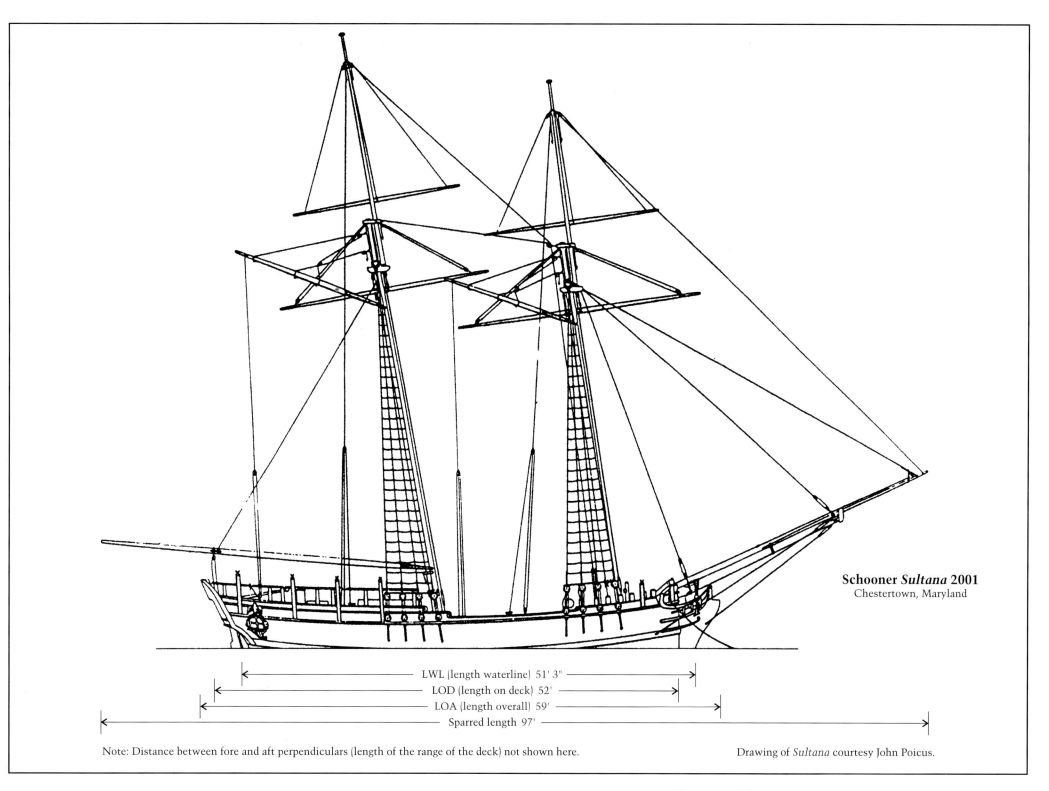

Schooner *Sultana* 2001
Chestertown, Maryland

LWL (length waterline) 51' 3"
LOD (length on deck) 52'
LOA (length overall) 59'
Sparred length 97'

Note: Distance between fore and aft perpendiculars (length of the range of the deck) not shown here.

Drawing of *Sultana* courtesy John Poicus.

# Notes

*Some logbook excerpts have been edited by the author. Where language usage and spelling errors do not impede understanding, logbook entries have been quoted as they were written, errors included.*

**Chapter 2. July 1768: John Inglis Takes Command**

1. Inglis's first day: *The Logbook of Lieutenant John Inglis, Commander of Sultana, 13 July 1768 to December 7, 1772*, PRO, Adm. 51/4358: 5, 6, 7, 8, 9. Public Record Office: London, U.K. The first day listed in Inglis's log is 15 July 1768, though it is very possible that Inglis's first view of *Sultana* came prior to that date.

2. Inglis family biographical information: John Alexander Inglis. *The Family of Inglis of Anchindiary and Redhall.* Edinburgh: T. and A. Constable, 1914 (incomplete), see especially chapter 15, "Vice-Admiral John Inglis, R.N.," 130-78.

3. Ibid., 130.

4. Ibid., 130–7. John Alexander Inglis is able to reconstruct John Inglis's career with great detail through 7 February 1763 after which he states, ". . . for the next ten years he [John Inglis] disappears almost entirely from view. His name is not to be found in the Navy lists, and the references to him in his uncle's account books are too slight to show how he was employed. He reappears in 1773 at Redhall [the family home in Scotland]." Working backward from *Sultana*'s logbooks and muster books (see list of primary documents in bibliography) Kees de Mooy establishes that the John Inglis of *Sultana* and the Vice Admiral John Inglis described by John Alexander Inglis are the same person. In Pursuit of Revenue: The Exploits of His Majesty's Armed Schooner Sultana, 1768–1772. Chestertown, Maryland: Washington College, undergraduate thesis submitted April 2001. John Alexander Inglis was apparently unable to make the connection between John Inglis and *Sultana*.

5. *Sultana*'s location and disposition at Deptford: *The Logbook of Lieutenant John Inglis, Commander of Sultana, 13 July 1768 to December 7, 1772*, entry for 15 July 1768, records Sultana "moored alongside the sheer hulk at Deptford." *The Logbook of David Bruce, Master of SULTANA, 19 July 1768 to 7 December 1772*, PRO, Adm. 52/1455, Public Record Office: London, U.K., entry for 20 July 1768 records *Sultana* "Alongside the Beadford Hulk." Bruce also records getting the main and foremasts on board and stepping them on 20 July 1768.

6. *Sultana* measurements and relative size: For measurements see *The Draught of His Majesty's Schooner Sultana, her Body Taken off in Mr. Randall's Dock and as she was fitted here. . . 21 June 1768.* Drawings, negatives 4521-2, collection of the National Maritime Museum, London, U.K. For *Sultana*'s size in relation to the Royal Navy see David Lyon, ed. *The Sailing Navy List, All the Ships of the Royal Navy—Built, Purchased and Captured—1688–1860.* London: Conway Maritime Press, 1993.

7. *Sultana*'s origins in Boston: Letter: *Survey Results of SULTANA from the Navy Board, 2 March, 1768.* PRO, Adm. 106/3315, Public Record Office: London, U.K. The Royal Navy survey letter states that *Sultana* was "built at Boston, six months ago." This would place the schooner's completion date around September 1767. Regarding Sir Thomas Asquith and *Sultana*'s original purpose, see letter: *Admiralty Board Orders to Survey SULTANA, 12 February 1768.* PRO, Adm. 2/237: 425, Public Record Office: London, U.K. The 12 February 1768 letter from the Navy Board states, "Sir Thomas Asquith having made a tender to us of a North American Schooner." Another document (letter): *From Rear Admiral Montagu Regarding SULTANA's Return to England, 8 October*

1772, PRO, Adm. 1/484, Public Record Office: London, U.K., states "the Schooner [*Sultana*] was built for a pleasure boat for a gentleman at Southampton but not answering to that purpose she was purchased for Government by orders of Sir Edward Hawke."

8. *Sultana*'s survey and refit by the Royal Navy: The condition of *Sultana* as she arrived in Deptford from Boston in 1768 is described in letter: *Admiralty Board Orders to Survey SULTANA, 12 February 1768*, which states that *Sultana*, "Appears to be well wrought and put together." Information about *Sultana*'s original rig and her rerigging by the Royal Navy was derived from several sources including Dana McCalip, *Some Thoughts on the Rigging of Colonial Schooners*. Nautical Research Journal 32, March 1986–1987: 30–6, and Harold M. Hahn, *The Colonial Schooner, 1763–1775*, Greenwich, England: Conway Maritime Press, 1981. The tally of fourteen sails was made by author Drew McMullen by cross-referencing the logs of John Inglis and David Bruce. The tally is an estimate. *Sultana*'s principal armament is described in the letter: *Navy Board Notice of SULTANA's Purchase and Recommendations for Manning and Arming*. 3 May 1768. PRO, Adm. 106/2199: 40, Public Record Office: London, U.K., which states that the schooner should be established with "Eight Swivel Guns." Both muskets and pistols are described in the logbook of John Inglis. Interior renovations including carpentry and masonry are described in *The Logbook of David Bruce, Master of SULTANA, 19 July 1768 to 7 December 1772*, specifically on 21 July 1768 when he records both carpenters and bricklayers at work.

### Chapter 4. September 1768: *Sultana* Crosses the Atlantic

1. *Sultana*'s position on 12 September 1768: The starting date for *Sultana*'s voyage across the Atlantic in the fall of 1768 is recorded as August 28 in *The Logbook of David Bruce, Master of SULTANA, 19 July 1768 to 7 December 1772*. Master Bruce also records *Sultana* as being 324 leagues from her starting point on 12 September 1768. The recorded position of the schooner on that day was 43°16′N, 21°33′W .

2. The loss of *Sultana*'s topsails: On 8 September 1768 Master Bruce records in *The Logbook of David Bruce, Master of SULTANA, 19 July 1768 to 7 December 1772*, "Hard gales and cloudy with rain, at 4 P.M. in balance reef of the mainsail and close reefed the foresail. Got down the topmasts and yards but in getting them down carried away both topsail yards in a hard squall."

3. *Sultana* takes on water: On 10 September 1768 Master Bruce records in *The Logbook of David Bruce, Master of SULTANA, 19 July 1768 to 7 December 1772*, "at noon shipped a great deal of water and the sea runs high."

4. Conditions belowdecks: Dimensions of the hold and crew compartments derived from *The Draught of His Majesty's Schooner Sultana, her Body Taken off in Mr. Randall's Dock and as she was fitted here . . . 21 June 1768.* Drawing, negatives 4521–2, collection of the National Maritime Museum, London, U.K.

5. *Sultana* foundering and casting off the hogsheads: Lieutenant Inglis records on 12 September 1768 in *The Logbook of Lieutenant John Inglis, Com-* *mander of Sultana, 13 July 1768 to December 7, 1772*, "Strong gales and squally with rain brought too under the foresail. Shipped a great deal of sea. Obliged to heave overboard into the sea 12 half-hogsheads of beer to save the schooner from foundering."

### Chapter 6. October 1768: *Sultana* Patrols Boston Harbor

1. *Sultana*'s arrival in Halifax: *The Logbook of David Bruce, Master of SULTANA, 19 July 1768 to 7 December 1772*. On 24 October 1768 Bruce records in his logbook, "at 8 A.M. came to anchor with the small bower in 10 fathoms, veered to ½ cable and moored St. Georges Island SSE. . . . at noon received 4½ tons of water . . . read the Articles of War and abstract of the act of parliament for the better payment of seaman's wages." On 7 October 1768 Bruce gives *Sultana*'s position as 86 leagues NW1/4W of Sable Island, or at 40°52′N, 49°27′W. The schooner struggled the rest of the month to make landfall.

2. Ballast and departing Halifax with *St. Lawrence*: *The Logbook of Lieutenant John Inglis, Commander of Sultana, 13 July 1768 to December 7, 1772*. Lieutenant Inglis records in his logbook on 25 October, "Received 5 tons of Ballast." Interestingly Bruce records the event a little differently in *The Logbook of David Bruce, Master of SULTANA, 19 July 1768 to 7 December 1772*, "Received 4 tons of shingle ballast." Both Inglis and Bruce record sailing in company with the schooner *St. Lawrence* beginning on October 26.

3. *Sultana*'s environs in Boston: *The Logbook of David Bruce, Master of SULTANA, 19 July 1768 to 7 December 1772*. Bruce records on 8 November 1772, "Came to anchor with the best bower in Boston harbor in 3½ fathoms, veered to ⅓ cable. Castle Island SE and the body of Boston town NW 3 cable lengths. Found riding near his Majesty's ships Mermaid, Glasgow, Senegal, Bonnatta, Beaver and St. Lawrence schooner."

4. The troops arrive from England: *The Logbook of David Bruce, Master of SULTANA, 19 July 1768 to 7 December 1772*. Bruce records on November 10, "arrived 3 ships with troops." On 15 November 1768 Lieutenant Inglis records in *The Logbook of Lieutenant John Inglis, Commander of Sultana, 13 July 1768 to December 7, 1772*, "Saluted Commodore Hood in His Majesty's Ship Romney with the Gaspee schooner. A signal for all Lieutenants [to come] on board the Commodore ['s vessel]."

5. Landing the troops into Boston: *The Logbook of Lieutenant John Inglis, Commander of Sultana, 13 July 1768 to December 7, 1772*. Inglis records on 16 November 1768, "Cloudy with rain and mid and later strong gales and cloudy . . . manned ship for General Gage and Lord William Campbell the boats employed landing the troops into the town of Boston."

6. Desertion of Edward Cunningham: *Muster Tables of His Majesty's Schooner SULTANA, 1768-1772*, Crew lists, PRO, Adm. 36/7269, Public Record Office: London, U.K. Edward Cunningham's vital statistics, including age, birthplace, rank, and dates of service, as well as the location, date, and method of his departure (when he ran from the schooner) are recorded in *Sultana*'s muster books. The motivations and thoughts ascribed to Cunningham in this passage are a creation of the author.

**Chapter 8. July 1770: Inglis Meets George Washington**

1. Sailing directions to the Chesapeake: Arthur Pierce Middleton. *Tobacco Coast, A Maritime History of the Chesapeake Bay in the Colonial Era.* Baltimore, Maryland: Johns Hopkins University Press, 1953: 82. Middleton states: "The sailing directions for the Capes compiled by Lieutenant Inglis of HMS Sultana in 1772 directed the incoming mariner bound to Hampton Roads to verify his latitude by sounding, the channel or fairway carrying nine to twelve fathoms. When up with Willoughby Point, the navigator, according to Inglis, 'cannot fail of seeing the Mark tree bearing, W1/2N.'" Inglis's sailing directions are on record at the Library of Congress: Sailing Directions, 1739-78, British Museum Additional MSS, British Transcripts in Library of Congress, 27891.

2. *Sultana* aground: *The Logbook of Lieutenant John Inglis, Commander of Sultana, 13 July 1768 to December 7, 1772.* Inglis records on 21 July 1770, "lost the graplin and hawser warping the schooner off Hampton bar."

3. Desertions: *Sultana* crew information from *Muster Tables of His Majesty's Schooner SULTANA, 1768-1772.*

4. Sailing with HMS *Boston* up the Potomac: *The Logbook of David Bruce, Master of SULTANA, 19 July 1768 to 7 December 1772.* Bruce records on 18 July 1770 that *Sultana* is sailing, "in company with His Majesty's ship Boston." According to Bruce's logs *Sultana* remains with *Boston* for the schooner's trip to the Potomac. Bruce records on July 24 in the Potomac River, "received on board a pilot." Inglis records in *The Logbook of Lieutenant John Inglis, Commander of Sultana, 13 July 1768 to December 7, 1772,* on 21 July 1768, "going out of Hampton Roads to Potomac River as per orders."

5. *Sultana's* activities on the Potomac: All of *Sultana's* searches, including ports of origin, destination, vessel type, and cargo described in the text are per Inglis's entries in *The Logbook of Lieutenant John Inglis, Commander of Sultana, 13 July 1768 to December 7, 1772.*

6. Dinner with Washington: Bruce and Inglis's dinner with George Washington and Inglis's brother's connection with Washington are described in de Mooy's thesis, In Pursuit of Revenue: The Exploits of His Majesty's Armed Schooner Sultana, 1768–1772. Both Bruce's and Inglis's logbooks place *Sultana* near Mt. Vernon on 29 July 1770 but neither mentions Washington or his homestead. George Washington records in his personal journal dining with "Inglis" and "Bruce" on the evening of 29 July 1770. Washington's entry in his journal, as quoted by de Mooy, is as follows: "[July] 29. Captn. Ingles [sic], and his Master, Mr. Bruce and Mr. John West dined here. All of whom returned afterwards." See Donald Jackson, ed., *The Diaries of George Washington* 2, Charlottesville: University Press of Virginia, 1976: 250. De Mooy elaborates: "The editorial footnote concerning this entry surmises that 'Ingles' was probably Samuel Inglis, a Norfolk merchant, or that 'there was a Captain Inglis of the British Navy . . . but he visited Virginia only in the falls of 1769 and 1770.' The editors of George Washington's diaries relied on newspaper notices contained in the *Virginia Gazette* for this information, which did not place Inglis and the *Sultana* in the vicinity of Mount Vernon during this time. However, the log-

books of the *Boston* and *Sultana* confirm that it was Captain Inglis and Master David Bruce of the *Sultana* who dined with George Washington on July 29." The remainder of the account of Inglis and Bruce's dinner with Washington is solely the creation of the author.

**Chapter 10. January 1771: Newport Becomes a Hotbed**

1. The seizure of Thomas Roberts in Newport: The basic framework upon which the account in this chapter is built is recorded by Bruce in *The Logbook of David Bruce, Master of SULTANA, 19 July 1768 to 7 December 1771.* On 21 January 1771 Bruce writes, "the people employed in clearing the decks and loading all the swivels and small arms because the people of Newport threatened to board us and cut us off [the anchor] and to burn the schooner for taking Thomas Roberts out . . . [illegible] . . . he had run from the schooner [*Sultana*] two months before." *Sultana's* muster books, *Muster Tables of His Majesty's Schooner SULTANA, 1768–1772,* confirm Roberts's age, origins, dates of service, and previous desertion from *Sultana.* The narrative details of this account, other than the items drawn from Bruce's logbooks and the muster books as described above, are solely a creation of the author.

**Chapter 12. November 1772: *Sultana* Returns to England**

1. *Sultana's* activities on the Delaware: *The Logbook of David Bruce, Master of SULTANA, 19 July 1768 to 7 December 1771.* On 22 March 1772 Bruce writes, "Came to sail, gave chase to a schooner, at 9 A.M., carried away 6 feet of the head of the mainmast." According to Bruce *Sultana* made do with a broken mainmast until 7 April 1772 when the schooner went into Philadelphia. On April 8 Bruce writes, "got the new mainmast in and rigged him." Regarding the brig *Carolina* on 8 May 1772 Bruce writes, "employed in going down the Delaware River upon an information, at 7 came to anchor in 3 fathoms, boarded the Carolina brig and searched her . . . came to sail as also did the prize brig. Employed in turning up the Delaware River in company with the George tender, the midshipman and 6 men went onboard the prize." On May 9 Bruce continues, "fired at 5 boats full of men . . . they intended to rescue the brig Carolina." On May 14, Bruce writes, "in boarding the sloop Polly lost overboard Henry Black sailor."

2. Account of the *Gaspee* incident: Neil R. Stout. *The Royal Navy in America, 1760–1775.* Annapolis, Maryland: Naval Institute Press, 1973: 141–3.

3. *Sultana's* voyage to Boston: Dates and locations taken from *The Logbook of David Bruce, Master of SULTANA, 19 July 1768 to 7 December 1771.*

4. Inglis leaves America: John Alexander Inglis. *The Family of Inglis of Anchindiary and Redhall.* According to J. A. Inglis, Lieutenant Inglis never returned to North America.

5. *Sultana's* sale: Harold M. Hahn. *The Colonial Schooner, 1763–1775:* 59.

6. See John Alexander Inglis, *The Family of Inglis of Anchindiary and Redhall,* and Kees de Mooy, In Pursuit of Revenue: The Exploits of His Majesty's Armed Schooner Sultana, 1768–1772.

# Sources

## Primary Documents

Note: With the exception of *Sultana's* muster tables the following list of primary documents was compiled by Harold M. Hahn in *The Colonial Schooner, 1763–1775.*

*"The Draught of His Majesty's Schooner Sultana, her Body Taken off in Mr. Randall's Dock and as she was fitted here. . . 21 June 1768."* Drawing. Negatives 4521-2, Collection of the National Maritime Museum: London, U.K.

United Kingdom, Public Record Office. *The Logbook of Lieutenant John Inglis, Commander of SULTANA, 13 July 1768 to December 7, 1772.* PRO, Adm. 51/4358: 5, 6, 7, 8, 9.

———. *The Logbook of David Bruce, Master of SULTANA, 19 July 1768 to 7 December 1772.* PRO, Adm. 52/1455.

———. Muster tables of His Majesty's schooner *Sultana*, 1768-1772 (crew lists). PRO, Adm. 36/7269.

———. Admiralty Board orders to survey *Sultana*, 12 February 1768. PRO, Adm. 2/237: 425.

———. Survey results of *Sultana* from the Navy Board, 2 March 1768. PRO, Adm. 106/3315.

———. Admiralty Board orders to Navy Board for purchase of *Sultana*, 8 March 1768. PRO, Adm. 2/237: 494–5.

———. Navy Board notice of *Sultana's* purchase and recommendations for manning and arming, 3 May 1768. PRO, Adm. 106/2199: 40.

———. Admiralty orders for manning and arming, 4 May 1768. PRO, Adm. 2/238: 5.

———. Letter from Deptford Yard to Navy Board indicating *Sultana* ready to receive men, June 1768. PRO, Adm. 106/3315.

———. Admiralty Board letter directing *Sultana* be put into service, 13 July 1768. PRO, Adm. 2/238: 69.

———. Admiralty instructions for *Sultana's* provisioning, 13 July 1768. PRO, Adm. 2/238: 68.

———. Admiralty instructions to supply *Sultana* with brandy, 27 July 1768. PRO, Adm. 2/238: 88

———. Letter from Rear Admiral Montagu regarding *Sultana's* return to England, 8 October 1772, PRO, Adm. 1/484.

## Selected Bibliography

### Books

Alden, John R. *A History of the American Revolution.* New York: Da Capo Press, 1969.

Anderson, Fred. *Crucible of War.* New York: Knopf, 2000.

Bolster, Jeffrey W. *Black Jacks: African American Seamen in the Age of Sail.* Cambridge, Massachusetts: Harvard University Press, 1997.

Buel, Richard, Jr. *In Irons.* New Haven: Yale University Press, 1998.

Cahill, Robert Ellis. *New England's Riotous Revolution.* Peabody, Mass.: Chandler-Smith Publishing House, 1987.

Cook, Don. *The Long Fuse: How England Lost the American Colonies, 1760–1785.* New York: The Atlantic Monthly Press, 1995.

Dann, John C., ed. *The Nagle Journal: A Diary of the Life of Jacob Nagle, Sailor, From the Year 1775 to 1841.* New York: Weidenfeld and Nicolson, 1988.

Flannery, Tim, ed. *The Life and Adventures of John Nicol, Mariner.* 1822. Reprint, New York: Atlantic Monthly Press, 1997.

Hawke, David Freeman. *Everyday Life in Early America.* New York: Harper and Row, 1988.

Hearn, Chester G. *George Washington's Schooners: The First American Navy.* Annapolis, Maryland: Naval Institute Press, 1995.

Inglis, John Alexander. *The Family of Inglis of Anchindiary and Redhall.* Edinburgh: T. and A. Constable, 1914.

Jackson, Donald, ed. *The Diaries of George Washington.* Volume 2. Charlottesville, Virginia: University Press of Virginia, 1976.

Kaminkow, Marion, and Jack Kaminkow, eds. *Mariners of the American Revolution.* Baltimore: Genealogical Publishing Co., Inc., 1993.

Linebaugh, Peter, and Marcus Rediker. *The Many Headed Hydra: Sailors, Slaves, Commoners, and the Hidden History of the Revolutionary Atlantic.* Boston: Beacon Press, 2000.

Middleton, Arthur Pierce. *Tobacco Coast: A Maritime History of the Chesapeake Bay in the Colonial Era.* Baltimore, Maryland: Johns Hopkins University Press, 1953.

Phillips, Kevin. *The Cousins' Wars.* New York: Basic Books, 1999.

Quarles, Benjamin. *The Negro in the American Revolution.* Chapel Hill: The University of North Carolina Press, 1961.

Rediker, Marcus. *Between the Devil and the Deep Blue Sea.* Cambridge, U.K.: Cambridge University Press, 1987.

Rodger, N.A.M. *The Wooden World.* New York: W.W. Norton and Company, 1986.

Stout, Neil R. *The Royal Navy in America, 1760–1775.* Annapolis, Maryland: Naval Institute Press, 1973.

Tuchman, Barbara W. *The First Salute: A View of the American Revolution.* London: Sphere Books, 1989.

Wood, Gordon S. *The Radicalism of the American Revolution.* New York: Vintage Books, 1991.

## Articles

de Mooy, Kees. "In Pursuit of Revenue: The Exploits of His Majesty's Armed Schooner Sultana, 1768–1772." Undergraduate thesis, Washington College. Chestertown, Maryland: April 2001.

Hanes, Susan. "Beef, Beer and Bread: Food on the Sultana." Undergraduate paper, Washington College. Chestertown, Maryland: May 2000.

Porter, Mark. "1436 Days on the North American Station with the Crew of His Majesty's Schooner *Sultana*," October 24, 1768, to October 12, 1772. Undergraduate paper, East Carolina University. Greenville, South Carolina: 1999.

## Selected Technical and Construction Sources

### Books

Bass, George F., ed. *Ships and Shipwrecks of the Americas: A History Based on Underwater Archaeology.* New York: Thames and Hudson, 1996.

Biddlecombe, George. *The Art of Rigging Containing an Explanation of the Terms and Phrases and the Progressive Method of Rigging Expressly Adapted for Sailing Ships.* New York: Dover Publications, 1990.

Chapelle, Howard I. *The History of American Sailing Ships.* New York: Bonanza Books, 1935.

———. *The Search for Speed Under Sail, 1700–1855.* New York: Bonanza Books, 1967.

Chapman, Fredrik. *Architectura Navalis Mercatoria: A Facsimilie of the Classic Eighteenth Century Treatise on Shipbuilding.* New York: Praeger Publishers, 1971.

Crothers, William L. *The American-Built Clipper Ship, 1850–1856: Characteristics, Construction, Details.* Camden, Maine: International Marine, 1997.

Estep, H. Cole. *How Wooden Ships Are Built.* Cleveland, Ohio: The Penton Publishing Company, 1918.

Footner, Geoffrey M. *Tidewater Triumph: The Development and Worldwide Success of the Chesapeake Bay Pilot Schooner.* Centreville, Maryland: Tidewater Publishers, 1998.

Ford, Barbara, and David C. Switzer. *Underwater Dig: The Excavation of a Revolutionary War Privateer.* New York: William Morrow and Company, 1982.

Gilmer, Thomas C. *Pride of Baltimore: The Story of the Baltimore Clippers.* Camden, Maine: International Marine, 1994.

Goodwin, Peter. *The Construction and Fitting of the English Man of War, 1650–1850.* London: Conway Maritime Press, 1987.

Greenhill, Basil. *The Evolution of the Wooden Ship.* New York: Facts on File, 1988.

Hahn, Harold M. *The Colonial Schooner, 1763–1775.* London: Conway Maritime Press, 1981.

Henderson, J. Welles, and Rodney P. Carlisle. *Marine Art and Antiques: Jack Tar, A Sailor's Life, 1750–1910.* Suffolk, England: The Antique Collectors' Club, 1999.

Lavery, Brian. *The 74-Gun Ship BELLONA.* London: Conway Maritime Press, 1995.

Lees, James. *The Masting and Rigging of English Ships of War.* London: Conway Maritime Press, 1979.

Lever, Darcy. *The Young Sea Officer's Sheet Anchor or a Key to the Leading of Rigging and to Practical Seamanship.* London: John Richardson, 1819.

Lundeberg, Philip K. *The Gunboat Philadelphia and the Defense of Lake Champlain in 1776.* Basin Harbor, Vermont: Lake Champlain Maritime Museum, 1995.

Lyon, David, ed. *The Sailing Navy List: All the Ships of the Royal Navy—Built, Purchased and Captured—1688–1860.* London: Conway Maritime Press, 1993.

Marquardt, Karl Heinz. *Captain Cook's ENDEAVOR.* London, Conway Maritime Press, 1995.

———. *Eighteenth Century Rigs and Rigging.* London: Conway Maritime Press, 1992.

McGowan, Alan. *HMS VICTORY: Her Construction, Career and Restoration.* Annapolis, Maryland: Naval Institute Press, 1999.

Polded, Ricard. *Endeavor, A Photographic Journey.* South Fremantle, Australia: Fremantle Arts Centre Press, 1998.

Roberts, David H., ed. *Eighteenth Century Shipbuilding: Remarks on the Navies of the English and the Dutch from Observations made at Their Dockyards in 1737 by Blaise Olliver, Master Shipwright of the King of France.* Ashley Lodge, England: Jean Boudriot Publications, 1992.

Stackpole, Edouard A. *Figureheads and Ship's Carvings at Mystic Seaport.* Mystic, Conn.: The Maritime Historical Association, Inc., 1964.

Story, Dana. *Frame Up! The Story of Essex, Its Shipyards and Its People.* Barre, Mass.: Barre Publishers, 1964.

Wilbur, Keith C. *Pirates and Patriots of the Revolution: An Illustrated Encyclopedia of Colonial Seamanship.* Old Saybrook, Conn.: The Globe Pequot Press, 1984.

## Articles

Broadwater, John, ed. "Yorktown Shipwreck Archaeological Project: Final Report." Williamsburg, Virginia: Virginia Department of Historic Resources, 1997.

McCalip, Dana. "Some Thoughts on the Rigging of Colonial Schooners." *Nautical Research Journal* 32, (1986): 30–6.

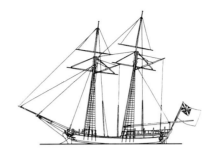

# The Schooner *Sultana* Project

# Index

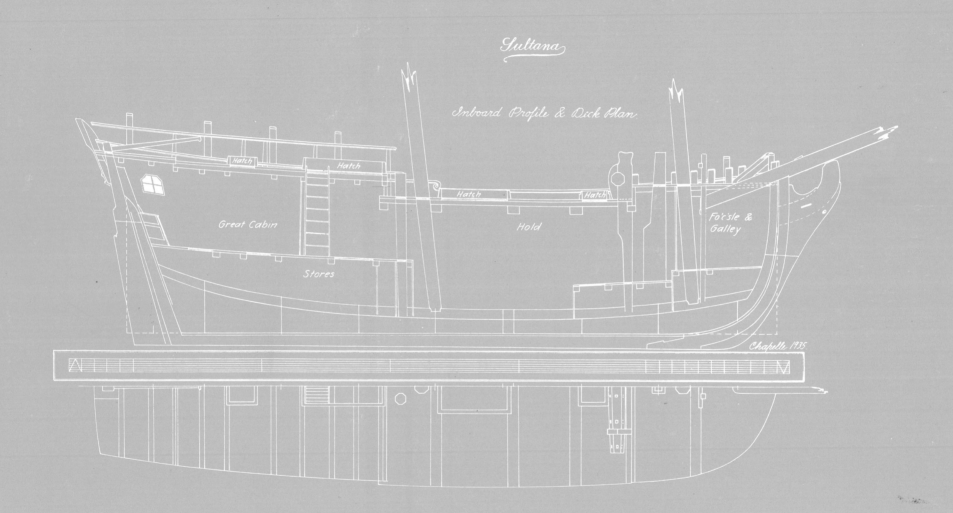

Sultana

Inboard Profile & Deck Plan

Great Cabin

Stores

Hatch

Hatch

Hatch

Hatch

Hold

Fo'c'sle &
Galley

Chapelle 1935